CALLED *to be* GOD'S LEADER

CALLED *to be* GOD'S LEADER

HOW GOD PREPARES HIS SERVANTS FOR SPIRITUAL LEADERSHIP

HENRY BLACKABY
&
RICHARD BLACKABY

THOMAS NELSON
Since 1798

NASHVILLE   DALLAS   MEXICO CITY   RIO DE JANEIRO   BEIJING

Published in Nashville, Tennessee, by Thomas Nelson. Thomas Nelson is a registered trademark of Thomas Nelson, Inc.

Thomas Nelson, Inc. titles may be purchased in bulk for educational, business, fund-raising, or sales promotional use. For information, please e-mail SpecialMarkets@ThomasNelson.com.

Unless otherwise noted, Scripture quotations are from THE NEW KING JAMES VERSION. Copyright © 1979, 1980, 1982, Thomas Nelson, Inc., Publishers.

Scripture quotations noted KJV are from the KING JAMES VERSION.

Published in association with the literary agency of Wolgemuth & Associates, Inc.

Library of Congress Cataloging-in-Publication Data

Blackaby, Henry T., 1935–
    Called to be God's leader : how God prepares his servants for leadership / Henry
Blackaby and Richard Blackaby.
        p. cm.
    Includes bibliographical references and index.
    ISBN 978-0-7852-8781-0 (trade paper)
    ISBN 978-0-7852-6203-9 (hardcover)
    1. Leadership—Religious aspects—Christianity. I. Blackaby, Richard, 1961– II. Title.
    BV4597.53.L43B56 2004
    253—dc22

                                                                        2004000783

Printed in the United States of America
08 09 10 QW 7 6 5 4

To my father,
G. R. S. Blackaby,
a dedicated and God-called layman, deacon, and businessman.
He was my first and major model for Christian leadership.

HENRY BLACKABY

To my three fantastic kids:
Mike, Daniel, and Carrie.
God is obviously molding your lives to be Joshuas of your day.
I am so proud of you!

RICHARD BLACKABY

CONTENTS

INTRODUCTION

FROM A HUMAN PERSPECTIVE, it can appear that great men and women have often pushed human progress forward both outside and inside the church. Moses freed God's people from slavery after Israel endured four hundred years in Egypt. Queen Esther saved God's people from obliteration. Paul was catalytic in bringing Christianity to the non-Jewish community outside of Judea and propelling it into an international movement. Augustine, Martin Luther, John Calvin, John Knox, John Wesley, and a host of others were key figures in church history. Their influence lives on generations later.

Yet it is a mistake to assume history is merely the summary of the efforts of great men and women. It is much more than that. It is the consequence of God's activity in peoples' lives. Brian Edwards concluded: "The point is that God has almost always used particular men to lead His work. That is His method."[1] History is largely the tale of how God used ordinary people to accomplish His extraordinary purposes throughout time.

The compelling question is: Why does God use some people for His purposes and not others? Does God not want His kingdom to expand in every place and in every age? Does He not intend for His will to be done on earth as it is in heaven? With so many people worldwide claiming to be Christ's followers, why does God not work mightily through each one? Would not such an overwhelming outpouring of God's power cause every knee to bow and every tongue to confess Jesus as Lord? Yet God does not work that way. He is selective in those He uses. When God places His hand upon a life, the effect is unmistakable. But many Christians today show little evidence of God's presence in their lives; consequently they fail to make a

> History is largely the tale of how God used ordinary people to accomplish His extraordinary purposes throughout time.

significant difference for God's kingdom. They live their lives without impacting their world. Tragically, this seems to be the norm for our generation. When God does work mightily through someone's life, it is the exception, and they become a celebrity.

It is fascinating to study the life of someone through whom God was pleased to work powerfully. Joshua lived thousands of years ago, yet the work God did through him continues to impact millions of people today. Everything changed once Joshua entered the scene.

In some ways, Joshua's life mirrors those of great secular leaders. Like Joshua, Julius Caesar's defining moment came after he crossed a river with his army. Both Caesar and Joshua had their Rubicon. And, like Caesar, Joshua could also conclude: "I came, I saw, I conquered."[2]

There are also striking parallels between Joshua and Winston Churchill. Churchill spent most of his life waiting in the wings of history for his moment to enter the world stage. He spent agonizing years in a political wilderness while others mismanaged his nation. When Churchill's countrymen finally called upon him in their greatest hour of need, he observed: "At last I had the authority to give direction over the whole scene as if I were walking with destiny, and that all my past life had been but preparation for this hour and for this trial."[3] Likewise, Joshua spent the greater part of his adulthood waiting. Yet, when finally called upon to lead, he accomplished the seemingly impossible and left his nation forever changed.

There are many similarities between Joshua and illustrious secular leaders, and we will make some comparisons throughout the book. We hasten to add that just because we draw parallels between Joshua and secular leaders such as Napoleon, Wellington, Nelson, and Elizabeth I, it does not mean we endorse or condone the spiritual or moral lifestyles of those people.

The crux of this book is that there was more to Joshua's success than personal giftedness, perseverance, or luck. His life was clearly directed by God. God's hand was powerfully upon him. God's wisdom skillfully guided him. His was a divinely lived life.

God still uses people today for His purposes and for His glory. God is no less capable of transforming our lives into His powerful instruments than He was with Joshua's life. The question is not about God's capability; it is about our availability. Are our lives as available to God as Joshua's was? Are we prepared for Him to make the necessary adjustments in us so His power is manifested through us?

God is no less capable of transforming our lives into His powerful instruments than He was with Joshua's life.

If there was ever a time when more Joshuas were needed, it is today. Many of God's people are in bondage. God's enemies appear ascendant on numerous battlefields in North America and around the world. Satan's strongholds seem invincible. Yet God is just as able to set people free and to defeat His enemies today as He was in Joshua's time. God continues to work through those who are willing to pay the necessary price to walk with Him as Joshua did. Our hope is that as you read this book, the Holy Spirit will awaken in your heart the passionate desire to settle for nothing less than God's best for your life and for those you lead. If you are not yet the leader you need to be, open your life afresh to God and let Him transform you into the spiritual leader He knows you can become.

God is no less capable of transforming our lives into His powerful instruments than He was wih Joshua's life.

ONE

LIMITLESS POSSIBILITIES

HIS WAS A HARD LUCK CASE. Forced to abandon his military career in disgrace, he subsequently experienced seven years of abject failure in the numerous businesses he attempted. As a farmer, real estate investor, rent collector, entertainment promoter, and entrepreneur, he grew repeatedly and intimately acquainted with bankruptcy. His applications to numerous local businesses were routinely declined. He was finally forced to sell his pocket watch, his only remaining valuable, to provide Christmas gifts for his impoverished family.

Reduced to peddling firewood on street corners, his ragged, unkempt appearance evoked pity from those who had known him in better days. When someone asked him why he was selling firewood in such humble circumstances, he replied, "I am solving the problem of poverty."[1]

Finally, in desperation, he took a job as a clerk working for his two younger brothers in a tannery. When war broke out, his application to join the army was rejected. Several futile attempts to enlist in the army prompted this lament: "I must live, my family must live. Perhaps I could serve the army by providing bread for them."[2]

It was an unlikely beginning for someone who would ultimately lead the Union armies to victory during the American Civil War and who, at age forty-six, would become the youngest man to be elected president of the United States. Yet such was the early life of Ulysses S. Grant.

The Bible tells of another man whose early life bore no hint of the great man he would become. Joshua's forefathers were slaves. Spanning four centuries, Joshua's ancestors had lived in Egypt, much of that time in bondage. Born with no possibility of freedom, education, or military training, the thought of a stellar military career would have seemed ludicrous to Joshua.

Joshua was an ordinary man who served a great God.

Yet he became a victorious general and even more importantly, a dynamic spiritual leader. The key to Joshua's astounding career was not found in his abilities or opportunities. Nor was it found in his character, though that was of sterling quality. The key was not found in Joshua at all. It was found in God.

History is most often viewed from a strictly human perspective, yet such a view is inherently incomplete. God is sovereign over history. Therefore, a study of any historical character must originate from God's viewpoint. To study Joshua as a great man would do a disservice to God and to Joshua. Joshua was an ordinary man who served a great God.

Joshua had many admirable qualities, but he also had flaws. Like everyone, he had his limitations. People, even "great" people are prone to failure. They can succumb to difficult circumstances. But words like *cannot* and *impossible* have no place in God's vocabulary (Rom. 8:31). From heaven's perspective, nothing is impossible (Luke 1:37). Likewise, when God sets a plan in motion, failure is not an option. These truths were made abundantly clear in Joshua's life despite humble circumstances.

GOD USED JOSHUA DESPITE HIS PAST

Details about Joshua's father are sketchy except that he was a slave from a long line of slaves. His name was Nun. Joshua's grandfather and great-grandfather were raised in bondage. It was their family business. It was all they knew. Generations of Joshua's ancestors grew up without the privileges most people take for granted. They were deprived of rights such as freedom of movement, access to education, possession of property, and respectful treatment.

Joshua's education was dictated by his position. A strong back was more useful than a keen mind. One can imagine Nun instructing his young son,

"Now Joshua, you are old enough to be working with the other men. Be careful not to look an Egyptian in the eye. That will get you a lash across your back. And don't ever be caught standing idle; it makes the taskmasters furious!"

Such childhood training would lead most Israelite children to grow up with few aspirations. At best, they could hope for a life with the fewest beatings possible and, God willing, the strength to endure each day. Such a lowly beginning was hardly what one would expect for a mighty general!

JOSHUA KNEW SUFFERING

Joshua undoubtedly grew up well acquainted with suffering. Thousands of years before workers' rights, legal protection, or public health care, a Hebrew slave's life would have been tedious, painful, and brief. The book of Exodus describes Egypt's cruel oppression of God's people. When God enlisted Moses to be His minister of deliverance for them, God said, "I have surely seen the oppression of My people who are in Egypt, and have heard their cry because of their taskmasters, for I know their sorrows" (Ex. 3:7).

Joshua quite likely saw those he loved whipped and beaten. Perhaps he helped tend their bloodied backs and watched the adults nursing their broken bones and rubbing their aching muscles. As he looked into his countrymen's eyes, did Joshua see the distant, hollow looks of those who had long-since lost any hope of their freedom? It's possible that among the sounds of moaning and weeping during the night's stillness, Joshua also overheard the hushed conversations of the adults wistfully describing their hope for the future and debating whether they would ever escape their misery.

What must have passed through young Joshua's mind as he watched the dreaded Egyptian soldiers racing past in their splendid chariots? Did Joshua remember that only a generation earlier, these soldiers had brutally massacred Hebrew babies in a crude attempt at population control? Was he mocked and mimicked by proud Egyptian boys as he passed them on the way to his work site? By the time Joshua was a teenager he had probably been taunted with every derogatory term in the Egyptian language. While Egyptian boys dreamed of becoming war heroes, victorious generals, and world travelers, what dreams did the slave boy Joshua harbor? Everything

3

about Joshua's world spoke of hopelessness. Yet did he dream, as young boys do, of a nobler life for himself and for his children?

STORIES FROM THE PAST

Whatever his dreams were, in reality his future looked bleak, and his present circumstances were equally dismal. Yet his distant past must have intrigued him. Hebrew parents would regularly recite the stories of their beginnings to their children. They would recount how, centuries earlier, God had encountered Abraham and told him to move his family from Haran to the land of Canaan. The adults would describe how Abraham trusted God's promise that one day his descendents would fill that land and be as numerous as the stars in the sky.

Everything about Joshua's world spoke of hopelessness.

They would relate how the revered patriarch Abraham, when he was one hundred years old, miraculously became a father. His elderly wife Sarah bore a son, Isaac. Isaac had two sons, Esau and Jacob. Despite Jacob's questionable beginnings, he, too, became a patriarch and God renamed him Israel. Jacob had twelve famous sons. God apparently had special plans for the eleventh son, Joseph. As a young boy, Joseph dreamed of one day being used mightily by God. Joseph's brothers grew jealous of their younger brother, so they sold him into slavery and exiled him to Egypt.

At this point in the story, young Joshua's heart must have quickened, for *he* was a descendent of Joseph. Regardless of how many times he heard the story, Joshua must have been thrilled to hear how Joseph rocketed from confinement in a dismal Egyptian prison cell all the way to an exalted and influential position at Pharaoh's right hand. When a famine forced Joseph's brothers to move their families to Egypt, Joseph became preeminent over them, just as God had foretold.

As the twelve sons of Jacob had children and enlarged their families, each of Jacob's sons' descendents became a tribe of Israel. Unlike the other tribes, however, God declared that Joseph's descendents would be so numerous as to form two tribes under his two sons, Manasseh and Ephraim. Both tribes would become powerful, but the descendants of the younger brother Ephraim would greatly surpass those from Manasseh's tribe. Joshua was from Ephraim's tribe.

Joseph's story may have seemed like a fairy tale to the young boys of Joshua's day. But it had happened. God had taken one of His children from the lowest position in society and elevated him to the highest. "If God did it once . . ." Surely the young Hebrew boys would have argued over which tribe was the greatest and speculated whether the distant prophecies concerning their tribes would ever become a reality.

The aged Jacob had prophesied of Joseph's tribe:

> Joseph is a fruitful bough, a fruitful bough by a well; His branches run over the wall. The archers have bitterly grieved him, shot at him and hated him. But his bows remained in strength, and the arms of his hands were made strong by the hands of the Mighty God of Jacob (from there is the Shepherd, the Stone of Israel), by the God of your father who will help you, and by the Almighty who will bless you with blessings of heaven above, blessings of the deep that lies beneath, blessings of the breasts and of the womb. The blessings of your father have excelled the blessings of my ancestors, up to the utmost bound of the everlasting hills. They shall be on the head of Joseph, and on the crown of the head of him who was separate from his brothers. (Genesis 49:22–26)

As young Joshua heard the elders reciting this prophecy, it may have seemed like a cruel joke. Yet the prophecy claimed that one day, Joseph's descendents would receive bountiful blessings from God. They would be valiant warriors with deadly bows. God Himself would strengthen the arms of their archers. Joshua was a direct descendant of the famous Joseph. Joshua knew the prophecy that his tribe, Ephraim, would one day be a mighty people (Gen. 48:19). Joshua's grandfather was Elishama, the chief of Ephraim (1 Chron. 7:26–27, Num. 1:10, 7:48). Yet, despite his

God's promises probably seemed as distant to Joshua as his dead ancestor Joseph.

5

prominent ties to Ephraim, God's promises probably seemed as distant to Joshua as his dead ancestor Joseph.

Winston Churchill may have experienced thoughts quite similar to Joshua's. Churchill's ancestor, John Churchill, was a successful general who had brilliantly saved England from her enemies. Having never lost a battle, he was named the first Duke of Marlborough. He established a splendid estate at Blenheim. Yet the Duke's coat of arms might have given a clue to his descendents' fortunes: it read "Faithful but Unfortunate." And so they were.

Over the years the Churchill family fortunes languished. Winston's father, Randolph Churchill, was a famed member of parliament but his political career, along with his health, painfully declined. Winston had experienced numerous setbacks by the time he came of age. He had failed miserably in school, receiving regular beatings from the principal. His father was too busy to spend time with him. Having no confidence in Winston's abilities, he suggested his son enter the army, since he was unlikely to succeed at law.

From this dubious beginning, Winston Churchill eventually became Britain's prime minister during his nation's greatest crisis. More so than any of his countrymen, he saved Britain from destruction and subjugation during World War Two. Heralded by many historians as the most influential leader of the twentieth century, young Churchill showed scant indication of his future accomplishments.

GOD USED JOSHUA DESPITE HIS YOUTH

In Joshua's day the Israelite people revered their elders. The elders made all the decisions. Joshua would have still been relatively young when the Exodus began. He would not have been considered a prominent national leader. Moses and his generation were the influential ones of that day. This may explain, in part, Joshua's initial silence when he returned from spying out the land with the other eleven spies. He and Caleb were in favor of immediately occupying the land of Canaan (Num. 13:30; 14:6–10).

When the minority report was given, however, the elder Caleb initially

spoke out rather than Joshua. And, when Joshua lent his voice to Caleb's pleas, rather than being persuaded, the people sought to kill him. Ironically, there would come a time when the Israelites would not question a word from Joshua, no matter how incredulous it might sound. However, in Joshua's youth this was not yet the case. Joshua still had much to learn and much to experience before the people would follow him unquestioningly. God was still shaping his young life.

> **Joshua still had much to learn and much to experience before the people would follow him unquestioningly.**

POSSIBILITIES REVEALED TO THE YOUNG

The Bible reveals a consistent pattern wherein God revealed to young men and women His plans to use their lives in a significant way. God gave young Joseph dreams of ruling over his brothers long before that revelation became a reality (Gen. 37:5–11). Samuel was consecrated to the Lord's service even before his conception (1 Sam. 1:11).

Likewise, God appointed the prophet Jeremiah for service before he was born (Jer. 1:5). Jeremiah hesitated to serve God because he was young, but God exhorted him, "Do not say, 'I am a youth,' For you shall go to all to whom I send you, and whatever I command you, you shall speak" (Jer. 1:7).

David was still a young shepherd boy when God alerted him that one day he would be a king (1 Sam. 16:12–13). Mary was still a teenager when she learned of God's incredible plans for her future (Luke 1:26–37). John was probably a young man when Jesus called him to follow Him. As the apostle Paul mentored young Timothy, he had to encourage his youthful protégé, "Let no one despise your youth" (1 Tim. 4:12).

Historically, God has repeatedly chosen young people and fashioned them into great leaders. The key for each of them, as it would be for Joshua, was their willingness to be patient and obedient as God prepared them for His purposes. At times emerging leaders limit their future possibilities by their impatience. They look for shortcuts to success, but God is methodical. He typically lays a foundation of character before building a superstructure of leadership.

GOD PROVIDES MENTORS

Another pattern found in Scripture is that God often provides significant mentors, teachers, and encouragers in individuals' lives to ready them for their future assignments. The aged priest Eli prepared young Samuel. Samuel worked with Saul. Elijah instructed Elisha. Joshua's primary teacher was Moses.

At times emerging leaders limit their future possibilities by their impatience.

There is no record of Joshua resisting Moses' leadership or resenting his instruction. Joshua apparently did not second-guess his leader. Rather, he accepted his role as assistant and zealously performed his assignments. Joshua obviously had faith in God's timing. He trusted God, not just in the abstract, but in his present circumstances. Because Joshua did not lose patience with God, he lived to enjoy a rewarding future, just as God promised.

Moses was a transitional leader. God used him to lead the Israelites out of Egypt to Canaan's doorstep. Yet Moses would not lead the people into the promised land. The next phase in God's plan would call on Joshua, the one who had been faithful during the transition time. Transitional periods can be difficult, especially for the young.

Like many young people, Joshua could have grown impetuous, anxious to move on to the next stage of his career. It would have been challenging to remain faithful to God and his assignment when things were in flux. No doubt Joshua pondered whether some of Moses' decisions were best. But, to his credit and to God's glory, he chose to be patient and glean all the wisdom he could from his elders, especially Moses.

GOD USES UNLIKELY CANDIDATES FOR LEADERSHIP

James MacGregor Burns observed that leaders often come from the "hinterland."[3] God takes pleasure in fashioning great leaders from the most unlikely candidates. Modern history corroborates the numerous biblical examples of God doing exactly that.

D. L. Moody was a poor, uneducated young man. His grammar was so poor, church members would squirm in their seats whenever he spoke up! He failed a simple entrance exam for church membership! Yet, by God's grace, he would become one of the greatest preachers of his era.

Billy Graham's first sermon lasted only eight 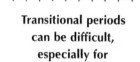 minutes! Those listening to his early attempts at preaching concluded he showed little promise for that vocation. Like Joshua, the early life of these men seemed to preclude any hope of success. Yet God is not as interested in our origins as He is in our obedience.

> **Transitional periods can be difficult, especially for the young.**

GOD USED JOSHUA DESPITE THE SINS OF OTHERS

Joshua's early life could be viewed from the perspective of abandonment. Many of the most significant people in his life left him. We must glean this in part from the silence of Scripture. Joshua's father, Nun, though named, is never described. There is no record of him teaching Joshua or giving him advice the way Moses' father-in-law counseled him (Ex. 18:13–27). We don't know if Nun was alive at the time of the Exodus. We can only assume that under the harsh working conditions, the life span of slaves was cruelly brief.

Did Joshua's father die while Joshua was still a young man, as Jesus' earthly father Joseph did? Could that be why God led Moses to adopt Joshua as his successor, bypassing Moses' own sons? If this is true, then God's work in Joshua's life is even more telling, since Joshua may have lacked the nurturing and support of a father during some of the most critical days of his life.

It is possible that Nun was alive during the Exodus. If so, this poses another problem, for Nun's generation committed a great sin against God by not trusting Him to lead them into the promised land. There is no record of Joshua's father speaking up in support of his son and Caleb after the twelve spies returned. This could indicate that either Nun had died by that time, or that he was among those who lacked faith in God.

If Nun was among the unfaithful generation, then Joshua would have had to suffer the anguish of wandering in the wilderness for forty years waiting for his own father to die, along with the other elders. Only then could Joshua

❀❀❀❀❀❀❀❀❀❀ move forward again. Seemingly either scenario—losing his father at a young age, or having an unbeliev-

God is not as interested in our origins as He is in our obedience.

ing father—meant Joshua had to rely upon the Lord for his guidance and strength in his faith.

Interestingly, Jesus lost His earthly father, Joseph, at a relatively young age. By the time Jesus

❀❀❀❀❀❀❀❀❀❀ entered His adult ministry, His father had apparently died and the only father Jesus could turn to was His Father in heaven.

LESSONS FROM HISTORY

A substantial number of history's famous leaders rose to greatness with little or no parental support. Alexander the Great grew up in the atmosphere of conspiracy and treachery as his father distanced himself from his son and was ultimately murdered. Winston Churchill's father had no time for his son, even when Winston pitifully begged for his attention. Horatio Nelson, the famed British admiral who defeated Napoleon's fleet at Trafalgar, was twelve when his mother died and his father, unable to care for his family, sent his young son to sea.

When the Duke of Wellington was a young boy, his family was sorely pressed for money. In an effort to improve their financial condition, they withdrew him from the prestigious school at Eton. His older brothers, Gerald and Henry, were allowed to remain because they showed more promise. The young duke's mother exclaimed, "I vow to God I don't know what I shall do with my awkward son Arthur. He is food for powder and nothing more."[4] Not a promising aspiration for the brilliant British general who would one day defeat Napoleon at Waterloo.

George Washington suffered a distant relationship with his mother and rarely visited her later in life. When Ulysses Grant was in dire financial straits, he wrote his father asking for a loan. His father never replied.

It is true that parental love and support is critical for a healthy upbringing, but God promises to be a "father of the fatherless" (Ps. 68:5). Joshua did not have many faithful role models among the elders and leaders of his people.

If anyone could have trusted God for miracles it should have been the

Hebrew leaders. They had seen God's fearsome ten plagues bring the mighty Egyptian empire to its knees. They had crossed the dry bed of the Red Sea and then watched the waters return to engulf the pursuing Egyptian army.

A substantial number of history's famous leaders rose to greatness with little or no parental support.

God had led them across the desert using a cloud by day and a pillar of fire at night. God miraculously provided daily food and water for an entire nation. Surely no generation ever witnessed such a spectacular array of miracles! Yet, when the twelve spies returned from staking out the promised land, the majority reported:

> "We are not able to go up against the people, for they are stronger than we." And they gave the children of Israel a bad report of the land which they had spied out, saying, "The land through which we have gone as spies is a land that devours its inhabitants, and all the people whom we saw in it are men of great stature. There we saw the giants (the descendants of Anak came from the giants); and we were like grasshoppers in our own sight, and so we were in their sight." (Numbers 13:31–33)

From that point on, things unraveled for the Israelites. The people degenerated to the point of worshiping a golden calf Aaron made for them out of their own jewelry. This generation composed the nation's leaders as Joshua emerged into adulthood. How easy it could have been for Joshua to embrace the faithless attitudes prevalent among the influential elders. He would have heard them discussing and justifying their desertion of God. Perhaps Joshua's own relatives were effusive in their reasons why God's will was impossible to follow.

Israel was not without its faithful spiritual leaders, but even they struggled. Moses, Joshua's revered leader disqualified himself from entering the promised land when he succumbed to his anger and disobeyed God's explicit command (Num. 20:1–13). Aaron and Miriam, two of God's most steadfast followers during Joshua's young adulthood, also paid a price for their disobedience. They had not been blameless and they would suffer the consequences

(Num. 12, 20:22–29). It must have disheartened Joshua to see his spiritual leaders fall by the wayside along with the rest of their generation. The indomitable Caleb would be the only elder to enter the promised land with Joshua.

How easy it could have been for Joshua to embrace the faithless attitudes prevalent among the influential elders.

Where did this leave Joshua? Those he had been raised to honor and respect were waffling in their faith and obedience. And, looking at the situation from a human perspective, they had good reason for their reluctance. Compared to the Canaanites, they were like "grasshoppers." Joshua had seen the terrifying enemy with his own eyes. Yet he chose to go against the prevailing consensus. Why? Perhaps he understood, like the apostle Paul, that one day he would give an account to almighty God for what *he* had done, and therefore he followed his convictions, even if he stood alone (2 Cor. 5:10).

ALONE IN OBEDIENCE

The Scriptures honor many men and women who, like Joshua, found themselves virtually alone in their obedience. Imagine being Noah, the only righteous person left on earth! (Gen. 6:8). Lot was the sole godly person living in Sodom (Gen. 19:15). Esther was the only believer in the king's household (Est. 2:10). Micaiah was the only prophet in Israel who prophesied what God told him rather than what the king wanted to hear (1 Kings 22:8). Job stood alone against the counsel of his friends and even his own wife. Such men and women are heroes of the faith, not because of any great performance of their own, but because they had the courage and good sense to trust God even as those around them did not. Joshua was one of those heroes.

Thanks to the Israelites' lack of faith, Joshua spent forty years wandering with them in the wilderness. Imagine what went through Joshua's mind when he heard God's edict pronounced to the people:

"As I live," says the LORD, "just as you have spoken in My hearing, so I will do to you: The carcasses of you who have complained against Me shall fall in this wilderness, all of you who were numbered, according to your entire number, from twenty years old and above. Except for Caleb the son of Jephunneh and Joshua the son of Nun, you shall by no means enter the land which I swore I would make you dwell in. But your little ones, whom you said would be victims, I will bring in, and they shall know the land which you have despised. But as for you, your carcasses shall fall in this wilderness. And your sons shall be shepherds in the wilderness forty years, and bear the brunt of your infidelity, until your carcasses are consumed in the wilderness. According to the number of the days in which you spied out the land, forty days, for each day you shall bear your guilt one year, namely forty years, and you shall know My rejection. I the LORD have spoken this. I will surely do so to all this evil congregation who are gathered together against Me. In this wilderness they shall be consumed, and there they shall die." (Numbers 14:28–35)

God certainly did not break the news gently! The Israelites, of all people, should have been primed to obey God. He had shown His power to them in every way imaginable, proving His trustworthiness. Now His words of reprimand to them were devastating. How heart wrenching to hear that God's will for you is for you to die! How pathetic the wails and sobs would have sounded as they rang out across the desert.

Surely Joshua was moved to see his uncles and aunts weeping under the weight of God's punishment on them. How pitiful it must have looked as the recalcitrant Hebrews strapped on their swords the next morning, determined to do, albeit belatedly, what God had told them to do in the first place. Despite Moses' warnings that neither he nor God would go with them, they foolishly assumed that since they were now ready to obey God's command, God would reverse His judgment upon them.

They were about to learn a difficult lesson: people leave God on their terms, but they must return on God's terms. Joshua must have watched with heavy heart as the humiliated Israelite survivors trudged

He followed his convictions, even if he stood alone.

back into camp, soundly defeated by the Amalekites and the Canaanites (Num. 14:39–45).

GOD USED A TRANSITION TIME IN JOSHUA'S LIFE

People leave God on their terms, but they return on God's terms.

We cannot underestimate the profound impact wandering forty years in the wilderness would have on Joshua. He had been ready and willing to enter the promised land immediately. But, because of someone else's sin, Joshua would have to delay God's will for his own life by forty years. This could have been an unproductive and wasted time, but Joshua chose to spend it walking with God, and time spent with God is never wasted.

Joshua experienced four decades of life lessons as he lived through the punishment, alongside the guilty ones. Could there have been any more graphic lesson on the perils of disobeying God? For forty years Joshua witnessed firsthand the consequences of disobedience. Joshua would attend burial after burial knowing what might have been, had that person only trusted the Lord. As even the great leaders Aaron, Miriam, and Moses all remained outside the promised land, Joshua must have determined in his heart never to accept less than God's best for his life.

As he paid the price for their sin, Joshua could not have helped but contemplate the failures of his predecessors. Most great leaders have been students of history. General George Patton observed: "You don't study history just to learn the dates. You study history to learn what to do right and what to do wrong."[5]

POSSIBILITIES IN THE DESERT

Did Joshua seek times of solitude in the desert, trying to understand why God would deal so severely with disobedience? What about Moses? Such a mighty man of God, yet he too was punished for his disobedience and irreverence. Could Joshua escape the truth that no person, not even one who had been used to part the Red Sea, was exempt from accountability to almighty, holy God?

Did Joshua develop a prayer life during those wilderness wanderings that would be his lifeline to God when he was leading the army? Did Joshua use that time to develop the personal habits of meditation and moral purity that would characterize his later life? Did God clearly and unmistakably assure Joshua of His purposes for him during that time?

Whereas Moses argued and resisted God's will for him, Joshua appears to have a stolid resolve throughout his time of leadership. Could it be that after communing with God for forty years in the wilderness, all his doubts and concerns were resolved? Clearly Joshua did not waste this time. While others were merely passing their days, Joshua emerged as a national leader. After four decades he was well prepared to boldly lead his people against numerous and seemingly insurmountable challenges.

For forty years Joshua witnessed firsthand the consequences of disobedience.

CONCLUSION

Some people inherit leadership positions. Others earn them. Joshua was certainly one of the latter. Nothing came easy for him. Joshua's initial slavery was not caused by his own failure, but by the decisions others had made centuries earlier. Likewise, Joshua's long years in the desert were not penance for his own sin, but payment for others' failures. A lesser man would have become bitter, but Joshua was wiser than that.

He couldn't always choose his circumstances but he could choose his response to them. Wise leaders refuse to let crises crush them. They use obstacles for their advantage. Times of waiting can be agonizing for a leader. Joshua made the most of his transition time. He didn't squander the years muttering about missed opportunities. He seized the opportunities God granted him. Most importantly, he never neglected his own walk with God. Because of his faithfulness he retained his hope.

Joshua faced hardships and disappointments largely foreign to us, yet he

Some people inherit leadership positions. Others earn them.

allowed God to interpret those circumstances for him. He faced the same travails that caused the demise of thousands of others, but he grew stronger as a result.

We have the opportunity to do the same thing. Success does not hinge on our heredity but on our heavenly Father. It does not depend on what others do but on what *we* choose to do. An effective life is not a matter of golden opportunities and lucky breaks. True success is determined by how we respond to the circumstances God allows us to experience.

God can use your life significantly, just as He used Joshua's. The question is: Are you prepared to let Him?

LIMITLESS POSSIBILITIES

- God used Joshua despite his past.
- God used Joshua despite his youth.
- God used Joshua despite others.
- God used transition times in Joshua's life.

QUESTIONS FOR CONSIDERATION

1. Does your past seem to mitigate against God using you in a significant way for His purposes? How about your current situation? How are you responding to those circumstances?

2. Are you presently in a time of transition? Are you making good use of your time? How will you be a better person after the transition?

3. What have you learned from watching the mistakes of others? Are there particular people whose lives stand out as a graphic warning to you? What warnings do their lives provide?

4. Are you currently waiting on the Lord for something? Are you demonstrating patience? What is God teaching you through this time?

TWO

SEIZING MOMENTS
TO BE FAITHFUL

HIS ASPIRATIONS WERE TO BE A SOLDIER. Yet his early career was fraught with disappointment and failure. On his first military assignment he inadvertently ambushed a group of foreign soldiers which helped set off a seven-year war. During that conflict, this ambitious soldier was ordered to establish an advance post in enemy territory. He chose his position so poorly that he had to surrender it almost immediately along with a regiment of his soldiers.

Later he served as a general's aid, but when the general followed his advice, his army suffered one of the most humiliating and decisive defeats in its history. When he was commissioned to take reinforcements to a fellow officer, he was mistaken for the enemy. They proceeded to fire on his soldiers and before they realized their mistake, forty of his men lay dead or wounded.

So unsuccessful was his early military career that he declared: "I have been upon the losing order ever since I entered the service."[1] In light of such an unpromising beginning it is understandable that George Washington was hesitant to accept command of all the American forces during the American Revolution. In his acceptance speech he declared: "I beg it may be remembered by every gentleman in the room that I this day declare with the utmost sincerity I do not think myself equal to the command I am honored with."[2]

POSSIBILITIES THROUGH FAITHFULNESS

The founding fathers of the American republic recognized that although Washington felt inadequate for the task and although he had not yet established himself as a successful general, he had faithfully and diligently undertaken all of his assignments. Washington had spent many years toiling for his country. He had suffered numerous defeats and setbacks. He had faced enemy fire on several occasions. During the disastrous defeat under General Braddock, Washington had four bullets pass through his coat.

> The most basic lesson in spiritual leadership: if you are faithful in a little, God will entrust you with more.

Anyone who met Washington was impressed with his bearing. He conducted himself as a veteran soldier who had always performed his duty. When the time came for his country to assign one of the greatest military commands in its history, it seemed prudent to choose him.

Some aspiring leaders constantly seek "the big break." They distribute their résumés, applying for important and prestigious positions. They use political tactics to gain friends and forge alliances. Sadly, those seeking to serve God often follow the same pattern. In so doing, they neglect the most basic lesson in spiritual leadership: if you are faithful in a little, God will entrust you with more (Matt. 25:21; Luke 16:10).

Faithfulness was fundamental to Joshua's success. More importantly, God was the key to Joshua's success. God relates to people on the basis of a covenant or promise. God said He would respond to obedience in one way and to disobedience in another (Deut. 27:11–28:68). When people trust in Him, He rewards their faithfulness, sometimes in miraculous ways. When people refuse to believe Him, they miss out on what God would have done and they face His discipline.

Only God knows what *could* have been with Joshua's peers had they obeyed God's revealed will for them. But Joshua was different. He was faithful so he experienced God's hand of blessing and power in everything he did. Step by step, Joshua's obedience led him to the top leadership position of his nation.

Joshua did not apply to be Moses' assistant. God chose him. When Moses asked God who should lead the people, God appointed Joshua:

> Then Moses spoke to the LORD, saying: "Let the LORD, the God of the spirits of all flesh, set a man over the congregation, who may go out before them and go in before them, who may lead them out and bring them in, that the congregation of the LORD may not be like sheep which have no shepherd." And the LORD said to Moses: "Take Joshua the son of Nun with you, a man in whom is the Spirit, and lay your hand on him; set him before Eleazar the priest and before all the congregation, and inaugurate him in their sight. And you shall give some of your authority to him, that all the congregation of the children of Israel may be obedient. (Numbers 27:15–21)

GOD'S ASSIGNMENTS

Joshua never set out to climb the ladder of success, nor did he pursue a career path in leadership. He did not assess his giftedness and decide on a military career. He served Moses because that was God's assignment for him. The initiative came from God. This truth would sustain Joshua during the darkest days when leading God's people was exceedingly difficult.

Benjamin Franklin said, "God helps those who help themselves." This slogan serves as a mantra for many people because it sounds "biblical" and it contains some truth. Joshua's life story demonstrates a different approach to life. It has been said of Ben Franklin that he "was never content to let opportunity find him."[3] Like so many others, he never lost an opportunity to further his career. He aggressively pursued what he wanted.

The people of our generation practice and promote the same attitude. People scheme and plan to improve their positions. They are commended as "industrious." They carefully monitor their salaries and benefits to ensure they receive maximum return for their efforts. They are viewed as "good money managers." They may achieve prominent positions, but these come through their own efforts.

His success was not "hard won." It was God given.

19

While they may take pride in their own achievements, they will never know the influence or satisfaction that comes from knowing God has appointed them to their positions. Joshua's life could certainly be labeled a success story, but his success was not "hard won." It was God given. The same is true of people like Joseph, Daniel, and David. They achieved significant success—even by worldly standards—but they didn't do it the world's way.

God set the agenda for Joshua's life and Joshua kept extremely busy responding in obedience.

Benjamin Franklin would have been more accurate to say, "God helps those who follow His will." The call for action is still there, but the efforts are initiated and accomplished by God rather than by our own scheming. If Joshua was anything he was a man of action. He did not sit around idly, waiting for God to do something. However, the key to Joshua's activity was God's will. God set the agenda for Joshua's life and Joshua kept extremely busy responding in obedience. His absolute faithfulness was evident long before he succeeded Moses.

JOSHUA: FAITHFUL FROM THE BEGINNING

First jobs can be quite telling. Emerging leaders don't often possess the expertise and skills that experience brings, but the attitude they bring to their first tasks can foreshadow how they will handle later responsibilities. Joshua's first major assignment was to lead the Israelite army against the hated Amalekites.

Amalek was Esau's grandson, born to Eliphaz and his concubine Timna (Gen. 36:12, 16). Esau had flatly rejected God's call on his life. Amalek chose the same path, with a vengeance. The nomadic Amalekites became the Israelites' archenemies. As the children of Israel traveled toward Canaan, the Amalekites attacked them.

Their assault was particularly odious because the Amalekites did not attack outright. Rather, they waited until the Israelites were exhausted from travel, then they ambushed the stragglers at the rear of the procession. Cutting down the weak and helpless was viewed as particularly cruel (Deut. 25:17–19). In response, Moses directed Joshua to mobilize soldiers and counterattack (Ex. 17:8–16). "So Joshua did as Moses said to him" (Ex. 17:10).

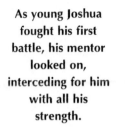

As young Joshua fought his first battle, his mentor looked on, interceding for him with all his strength.

Moses surveyed the skirmish from the crest of a hill as Joshua led the assault against the enemy. As long as Moses held up his arms in intercession for Joshua and his forces, the Israelites prevailed (Ex. 17:11). When Moses' arms grew weary and he was forced to lower them, the Amalekites gained the advantage. God provided a wonderful picture of an older statesman undergirding an emerging leader. As young Joshua fought his first battle, his mentor looked on, interceding for him with all his strength.

Once the battle was won, Moses built an altar and named it, "The Lord is my banner" (Ex. 17:15). Moses was signifying that God had fought for them against their enemies. Joshua had successfully completed his first major assignment and he had come to know indeed what it meant for God to intervene on his behalf. Centuries later these same Amalekites would be the undoing of another young leader, King Saul, because Saul chose to disobey God's directive (1 Sam. 15; 2 Sam. 1:13–16).

JOSHUA: FAITHFUL TO HIS NAME

Have you ever heard of Hiram Grant? Probably not, but when young Grant applied to West Point, his father sought the aid of Congressman Thomas Harder. In Harder's haste to request the appointment, he mistakenly listed Hiram Ulysses Grant's name as Ulysses S. Grant.[4] Despite Grant's later attempts to correct his name in the military records, history would bring fame and significance to a name that was not really his.

In Old Testament times, a Jewish person's name was significant because it was considered a reflection of one's character. The Scriptures show that when God personally encountered people, He often changed their names to reflect His will for them. Abram and Sarai became Abraham and Sarah to signify that God would establish a nation through them (Gen. 17:5, 15).

❦❦❦❦❦❦❦❦❦❦

**A new title does
not ensure a new
character—
obedience does.**

❦❦❦❦❦❦❦❦❦❦

Jacob's new name was *Israel*, meaning "God strives," to match God's work in his life (Gen. 32:28). Rather than remaining a trickster and a conniver, he would become a patriarch of God's people. Jesus changed Simon's name to *Peter*, "a rock," to match the sturdy character God would develop in him (John 1:42).

While a name change often signaled an immediate role change, it did not automatically mean an instant alteration in character. That would come through obedience, as individuals allowed God to stretch them to match their new identities. For example, the Bible indicates that, by name, Christians are children of God, yet not every Christian behaves like God's heir (Rom. 8:14–17). The degree to which Christians assume the characteristics of their new identity is up to every believer. Likewise, the Bible refers to those redeemed by Christ as saints (Rom. 1:7). But living a saintly life is a choice each Christian makes personally. A new title does not ensure a new character—obedience does.

It was a highly meaningful act when God altered someone's name. When God renamed Joshua (from Hoshea), the difference was significant (Num. 13:16). *Hoshea*, meaning "He has saved," was a good, respectable name. *Joshua* meant "Yahweh saves."

God moved from generalities to specifics. *Hoshea* did not refer to a particular god. In an age of rampant idolatry, the name could have referred to any of the numerous false gods. But *Joshua* specified the one Lord God. It was personal. And indeed, Joshua would come to experience God in an increasingly personal way. The name change was subtle, but the difference was profound. *Hoshea* had a religion. *Joshua* had a relationship with God. For the rest of his life, Joshua pursued God's call to a relationship rather than merely becoming a religious leader.

CALLING OR CAREER?

What is the difference between pursuing a calling and building a career? Richard Nixon's life demonstrates the latter. He grew up in poverty. He

22

recalled often having nothing more than cornmeal for dinner. Due to his diligence at school, Nixon was offered a scholarship to Harvard Law School in Massachusetts. However, he had to decline it. He could not afford the travel home to California to help his parents during his breaks in classes.[5] At one point while Nixon was in Whittier College he moved into a toolshed to save money.

> For the rest of his life, Joshua pursued God's call to a relationship rather than merely becoming a religious leader.

As a teenager Nixon was not popular and this troubled him. In fact, he battled insecurity all his life. He found it almost impossible to trust people. Perhaps that's because he justified using questionable means himself if they furthered his own interests. When he was anxious about his academic standing, he broke into the dean's office to learn his final grades.[6] In the political arena, he used dubious means to win elections and to gain influence.[7]

His aggressive approach to getting what he wanted ultimately led him to become vice president of the United States, serving under President Dwight Eisenhower. It seemed a clear path to the Oval Office. Yet Eisenhower struggled with his associate. He recognized that Nixon had the skills and intelligence to be a national leader, but Eisenhower was concerned that Nixon never seemed to grow in his character. Eisenhower's secretary, Ann Whitman, observed, "The president is a man of integrity and sincere in his every action . . . He radiates this, everybody knows it, everybody trusts and loves him. But the vice president sometimes seems like a man who is acting like a nice man rather than being one."[8]

Even Nixon himself knew he fell short. Interestingly, once he was elected president, he made numerous resolves to develop his character to a level appropriate for a national leader. Ironically, his goal for the year 1971–1972 was "President as moral leader."[9] Yet his fundamental inability to trust people quickly revealed itself. After only twenty-seven days in the White House, Nixon described the media to an aid: "You don't understand, they are waiting to destroy us."[10]

Yet neither his repeated resolutions nor his friendship with respected spiritual leaders, including Billy Graham, brought change. Nixon persistently suspected others and continually questioned their motives. He isolated himself from others. He suffered paranoia, convinced that those around him were plotting his downfall. Even as he headed toward a landslide re-election victory in 1972, the president constantly sought questionable, covert means to undermine and defeat his opponents.

✤✤✤✤✤✤✤✤✤✤✤ Nixon ultimately achieved his childhood dream, but the Watergate scandal would bring it crashing down in nightmarish proportions. He had the savvy to attain his lofty career goals, but he never allowed God to develop his character to match his enormous responsibility. His story is infamous, but not uncommon. It is tragic whenever people pour their efforts into achievement rather than into their relationship with God. A leadership position without corresponding character inevitably leads to failure. Joshua built a relationship with God rather than a career and as a result, people are studying his life and influence thousands of years later.

> **A leadership position without corresponding character inevitably leads to failure.**

JOSHUA: A FAITHFUL BELIEVER

After a particularly discouraging military campaign early in his career, the Duke of Wellington observed that he had "learnt what not to do, and that is always something."[11] Leaders' reputations are not based solely upon what they *do*. What they choose *not* to do matters too.

When the Israelites reached Mount Sinai, Moses took Joshua up the mountain for an unforgettable experience (Ex. 24:13; 32:17–18). Scripture indicates: "The glory of the Lord rested on Mount Sinai . . . the sight of the glory of the Lord was like a consuming fire" (Ex. 24:16–17). Back at the foot of the mountain, Aaron and Hur were in charge for forty days while Moses and Joshua were gone (Ex. 24:14). During Moses and Joshua's sacred encounter with God, God gave Moses the Ten Commandments. He also laid out detailed instructions concerning proper worship and sanctified behavior.

Meanwhile, without their leader, those who remained behind grew restless and agitated. One of the greatest failures in biblical history unfolded as the Hebrews exhorted Aaron, God's priest, to make for them a god they could see and worship. He reluctantly took their gold and fashioned it into a golden calf (Ex. 32:1–6). In spite of witnessing God's mighty judgments on their enemies and after experiencing His miraculous provision themselves, the Israelites willingly abandoned the true, living God for a lifeless statue. What an incredible affront to almighty God!

A WILLING SPIRIT

The contrast between Aaron and Joshua is telling. We never read of Joshua bowing to the people's pressure. Aaron, however, seems to have been easily swayed. When ten of the twelve spies argued against entering the promised land, there is no record of Aaron speaking in favor of obeying God, as Joshua did, yet Aaron was God's appointed spokesman (Ex. 4:14–16). He was a gifted speaker. One could imagine him rousing the crowds to do what was right, much as Demosthenes brilliantly exhorted his fellow Athenians or Cicero challenged his Roman countrymen. But Aaron apparently remained silent when he should have pointed the people back to God.

Conversely, Joshua is not portrayed as an eloquent orator, yet he never failed to speak up as a spokesman for God. The truth is, eloquence without obedience is worthless. In fact, it's dangerous. God proved through Joshua and through countless other great leaders that a willing spirit is what He looks for when doing His mighty work. Perhaps Joshua's awareness that he was *not* a gifted speaker led him to rely completely upon the Lord and thus, to be such an effective leader.

> **Eloquence without obedience is worthless. In fact, it's dangerous.**

GOD CHOOSES CHARACTER

Why did God allow Joshua to accompany Moses up the mountain? (Ex. 24:12–13). Did the aged Moses need Joshua to care for him as he met with God? Whether or not Moses needed Joshua, God must have wanted Joshua

25

to experience a life-changing encounter with Him as Moses did. Joshua would need an intimate walk with God to carry out the enormous assignment awaiting him.

God gives assignments to those who have the character to handle them. God had an incredibly challenging assignment for Joshua so He fashioned his character accordingly, partly through Joshua's presence on the mount. That profound moment on the mountaintop set the tone for a lifelong intimacy between God and Joshua.

God gives assignments to those who have the character to handle them.

Every encounter with God opens up limitless possibilities. No one leaves an encounter with God unchanged. Certainly Joshua did not. Perhaps the sound of God's voice rang in Joshua's ears for the rest of his life. Did Joshua often recall the fire, thunder, lightning, and smoke that engulfed the mountain during those terrifying days? Did the experience so overwhelm Joshua that he could never doubt God afterward? Did the encounter so terrify Joshua that he feared God's wrath until the day he died?

Undoubtedly, Joshua's divine meeting on Mount Sinai was a watershed experience that defined the rest of his life. His presence with Moses provided this opportunity and his absence from among the rebellious Israelites saved him from the ungodly turn of events unfolding at the base of the mountain.

Sometimes where we are *not* is as important as where we are. Had Joshua been among the rebellious Israelites, it seems doubtful he would have compromised his faith as Aaron did. He might have once again stood firm against the tide of apostasy. He might even have been martyred for his righteous stand. Aaron's resolve proved insufficient in his time of testing.

Soon it would be Joshua's turn to rise up as a spiritual statesman, but this time instead of testing his faith God was profoundly strengthening it. None of us knows how often God has spared us in a similar way, but sometimes hindsight affords the wisdom to look back and thank God for preserving us from temptation and tragedy.

GOD'S PROTECTION

Henry's father, Gerald Blackaby, was a devout Christian who served in the Canadian military during World War One. He was a machine gunner in numerous battles. Once he was briefly called away from his trench and returned to find a large crater where he had just been crouching. His fellow soldiers were astonished to see him alive!

Another time, he was preparing for a charge across no man's land when his weapon malfunctioned. As he stopped and struggled to fix it, a comrade offered to take his place in the front ranks. The soldier leaped out of the trench and an enemy bullet immediately struck him down. These and other dramatic moments in Blackaby's life made him keenly

Sometimes where we are *not* is as important as where we are.

aware God was protecting him for a purpose. He spent the rest of his life faithfully serving God, leading numerous people to Christ and helping to start several churches.

Henry and his two brothers grew up with the knowledge that God had unique plans for their family. Now the third generation is grown and they are passing on the rich Christian heritage to their children. Though the senior Blackaby has been gone for many years, he would be so pleased to know his grandchildren are faithfully serving his Lord—eight in full-time Christian ministry. And now his oldest great-grandchild, Mike Blackaby, is in seminary responding to God's call on his life.

Joshua always knew God had called him for a special purpose to serve Him and to bring honor to His name. And Joshua spent a lifetime doing exactly that. As a result, he lived in a way that always demonstrated his absolute trust in God and always brought glory to God.

JOSHUA: FAITHFUL IN THE MINORITY

The Israelites were camped at Kadesh Barnea, bordering on the promised land. It was time for a reconnaissance mission to survey the territory before their initial attack (Num. 13:1–2). Under God's instructions, Moses chose one influential leader from each tribe for this momentous enterprise. It says much about Joshua that he was selected (Num. 13:8). Ephraim was a populous tribe; a large number of ambitious young men and respected older leaders were no doubt prepared to take on the assignment.

This was an exciting but dangerous mission. The land was allegedly occupied by malevolent giants. Large, formidable fortresses guarded the main roads. Capture, torture, and death were all distinct possibilities. The mission was also of great strategic significance. The twelve spies would gather critical information to determine which route the invading Israelites would take in their conquest. The nation's future rested on the success of a dozen scouts.

Of course, the spies' report is infamous now. First, they confirmed Canaan was everything God promised: "We went to the land where you sent us. It truly flows with milk and honey, and this is its fruit" (Num. 13:27). They were, to a man, impressed with the land, but ten of them were intimidated by what else they saw:

> Nevertheless the people who dwell in the land are strong; the cities are fortified and very large; moreover we saw the descendants of Anak there. The Amalekites dwell in the land of the South; the Hittites, the Jebusites, and the Amorites dwell in the mountains; and the Canaanites dwell by the sea and along the banks of the Jordan. (Numbers 13:28–29)

Yes, the land was beautiful, but immense obstacles loomed before them. These men had personally witnessed God's terrifying plagues on Egypt; they had watched God engulf the mighty Egyptian army with the Red Sea; they had seen God defeat the Amalekites en route; and they had miraculously received nourishment in the wilderness. Yet they doubted God's ability to give them victory this time.

In spite of a national history permeated with the mighty acts of God, ten of the spies assessed their situation from a human perspective. Their fear convinced them that conquering Canaan was impossible. It is a familiar pattern. Centuries later, Jesus would chastise His twelve disciples for their inability to trust Him in spite of all they had seen Him do: "'Do you not yet perceive nor understand? Is your heart still hardened? Having eyes, do you not see? And having ears, do you not hear? And do you not remember?' So He said to them, 'How is it you do not understand?'" (Mark 8:17–18, 21).

During World War Two, the outspoken American general George Patton said: "Cowardice is a disease and must be checked immediately, before it becomes epidemic."[12] Likewise, General Patton's boss, General Dwight Eisenhower, noted: "Optimism and pessimism are infectious and they spread more rapidly from the head downward than in any other direction."[13]

And so it was that ten of Israel's most respected leaders expressed their own unbridled fears and the result was pandemic. The people trembled in terror. As if to seal the matter, the spies reiterated: "The land through which we have gone as spies is a land that devours its inhabitants, and all the people we saw in it are men of great stature. There we saw the giants . . . and we were like grasshoppers in our own sight, and so we were in their sight" (Num. 13:32–33).

At this even the most stouthearted elders and warriors lost heart. It is not surprising that God later commanded Israelite military commanders to send home any soldier who was fearful of the enemy lest their cowardice infect their fellow soldiers (Deut. 20:8).

The tremor of fright spread through the mob like a prairie grassfire. They were united as one desperate voice in their shared anguish. Somehow, Caleb managed to quiet the crowd:

> "Let us go up at once and take possession, for we are well able to overcome it," Joshua and Caleb pleaded . . . "The land we passed through to spy out is an exceedingly good land. If the LORD delights in us, then He will bring us into this land and give it to us, 'a land which flows with milk and honey.' Only do not rebel against the LORD, nor fear the people of the land, for they are our bread; their protection has departed from them, and the LORD is with us. Do not fear them." (Numbers 13:30; 14:7–9)

Joshua and Caleb were overwhelmingly outnumbered. Panic paralyzed their countrymen. Their ten comrades, all influential leaders among their tribes, dashed icy water over any hope of success. Still Joshua and Caleb refused to back down. They risked death by stoning as they urged the mob to be faithful (Num. 14:10). They knew God would deliver them if only His people would trust Him. Such a stouthearted stand early in Joshua's life offers a glimpse into his character. He held fast to God's word, regardless of the cost. Strong spiritual leadership demands such integrity.

JOSHUA: FAITHFUL IN WORSHIP

He held fast to God's word, regardless of the cost.

"So the LORD spoke to Moses face to face, as a man speaks to his friend. And he would return to the camp, but his servant Joshua the son of Nun, a young man, did not depart from the tabernacle" (Ex. 33:11). The tent of meeting stood off in the distance, representing the place where God encountered His people. When Moses left the camp, heading for the special tabernacle, his short journey always caused a stir in the settlement. Each man would stand in the entrance to his own tent, watching Moses as he disappeared inside the meeting place. As Moses met with God, each man would worship the Lord in the doorway of his own tent (Ex. 33:8–11). When he returned, the radiant glow on Moses' face told everyone he had met with his Lord.

Apparently Moses came and went from God's presence in the tabernacle but Joshua, his faithful assistant, remained at the tabernacle. Joshua accompanied Moses to the meeting place but probably did not go inside with Moses. Since the meeting place was a tent, Joshua might have heard God's voice if it was audible. Even if he heard nothing, Joshua would have been aware of the poignancy of those moments. The effect on Joshua must have been profound. Centuries later, Jesus' conversations with His Father would similarly intrigue His disciples, propelling them to ask how they, too, could meet with God as He did (Luke 11:1).

Joshua apparently chose to spend many hours at the tabernacle. It is God who stirs the hearts of His people to want to draw closer to Him (John 6:44–45, 65). Obviously God was at work in young Joshua's life. Perhaps as

Joshua regularly witnessed Moses meeting with God, a growing desire to know God in a similar way swelled within Joshua's heart. Joshua was not content to merely watch others meet with God. He may have dreamed of the day when he would enter the tent as well and meet with God personally.

Joshua's tenacity is noteworthy. He stayed longer at the worship site, but his countenance was not changed as Moses' was. The senior leader enjoyed the spiritual intimacy that comes from years of fellowship with God. There are no shortcuts to such a walk. Joshua was still getting to know the Lord and he wisely seized opportunities to spend time with Him.

While Joshua did everything he could to draw closer to God, God chose to manifest Himself to Joshua and the other Israelites in different ways. Despite Joshua's reverence for God, and despite the fact God spoke often to him, God never caused his face to glow as He did with Moses. This was God's doing. Perhaps God did not want to divide the loyalty of the Israelites between Moses and Joshua.

Sovereign God chose to establish a unique relationship with Moses. Likewise, the Israelites had to remain content with watching from the doorway of their tents as Moses went to meet with God. They had not been summoned into God's presence as Moses had. For them to attempt to force their way into God's presence without a divine invitation would have been fatal (Ex. 19:20–21).

Certainly, Joshua's role as a prominent leader would have given him numerous administrative duties to perform. We do not know all the mundane, time-consuming responsibilities that came with being Moses' right-hand man. Yet Joshua chose to spend every available moment in God's presence. Surely such an investment of time and effort by Joshua as a young man contributed to his lifelong unwavering walk with God. We would do well to emulate his devotion.

JOSHUA: FAITHFUL TO GOD'S WARNINGS

Joshua's close working relationship with Moses afforded him a good vantage point from which to observe his mentor's faithfulness. It also gave him a

❧❧❧❧❧❧❧❧❧❧

It is God who stirs the hearts of his people to want to draw closer to him.

❧❧❧❧❧❧❧❧❧❧

unique opportunity to learn from Moses' mistakes. For example, Joshua was present in the wilderness when God told Moses to speak to a rock so water would spring forth for the thirsty Israelites (Num. 20:1–13). But Moses, fed up and angry with his countrymen's murmuring, struck the rock rather than speaking to it as God instructed. Water did gush forth, but God solemnly pronounced: "Because you did not believe Me, to hallow Me in the eyes of the children of Israel, therefore you shall not bring this assembly into the land which I have given them" (Num. 20:12).

God would not tolerate such a display of disobedience even from a spiritual paragon like Moses. Moses' temper cost him immensely. We can only imagine Joshua's shock when Moses gave him the news. Joshua could surely understand why the rebellious Israelites were barred from Canaan. He probably agreed that grumblers like the sons of Korah should be punished for their insolence (Num. 16:1–40). Obviously Aaron, who crafted the golden idol, must suffer the consequences.

But Moses' offense must have seemed minor, especially in light of his faithful track record. Moses had delivered the Israelites from Egypt. He had called down ten plagues on the Egyptians and parted the Red Sea! He had ascended the terrifying Mount Sinai and received God's law. He had spoken with God face to face! Surely God would not deny him his heart's desire! Nonetheless, God charged Moses with treating Him irreverently before His followers. And so after forty years of leading God's people, Moses was forced to stop short of his heart's desire.

Imagine the conversations the two leaders shared as they discussed Moses' fate. Did the chagrined mentor urge his protégé to beware of making the same mistake? Did he exhort Joshua to follow God's instructions implicitly, no matter what the circumstances? The lesson for Joshua was clear: walking with God was not about a method; it was about a relationship.

Earlier God had instructed Moses to strike a rock and water had burst forth (Ex. 17:6). The next time the Israelites needed water, God instructed

Moses to speak to a rock. Perhaps Moses was too preoccupied with his anger to carefully note the specifics of God's instruction. Perhaps Moses merely resorted to the method that had worked for him the last time (Num. 20:8–12). Whatever the reason, he struck the rock twice instead of speaking to it as he had been instructed. It might seem like hair splitting, but God knows the heart and Moses' carelessness cost him dearly.

Walking with God was not about a method; it was about a relationship.

Both Moses and Joshua knew this wasn't the first time Moses' temper had gotten him in trouble. His choleric outburst against an Egyptian earned him forty years as a fugitive from Egyptian justice (Ex. 2:11–15). Moses' anger stirred him to destroy the original stone tablets upon which the Ten Commandments were written (Ex. 32:19, 34:4). Now his unchecked anger flared up to burn him again. One glance at the forlorn Moses may have turned Joshua's thoughts to the gravity of his own sins.

Joshua was on the receiving end of another golden opportunity—to learn from another's mistakes. To this day God allows people to be publicly and dramatically punished for carelessly disregarding His word. Their humiliation serves as a graphic warning to the rest of us. What a terrifying thing to be an object lesson of God's displeasure! (Heb. 10:31).

Perhaps young Joshua tried to comfort his friend. Perhaps he urged Moses to seek God's reversal of His edict. They both knew Moses had accomplished much in God's service. Surely God would take this into account. Yet, Moses knew God well. He was fully aware of God's holiness. God had every right to command the respect Moses had failed to give Him and Moses knew it.

God was also sending a stark message to the rest of the people—no one was beyond humble obedience to God. When Moses had pled with God to relent from His judgment, God finally commanded him to never ask again (Deut. 3:23–26). The specter of Moses' situation must have reminded all the people to reflect on their own desperate need to heed God's commands. Obviously *no one* was exempt from accountability to God. This poignant reminder would no doubt serve Joshua well in later years as he took on the role Moses had once held.

CONCLUSION

Joshua did not weasel and claw his way into anyone's favor. Not God's or man's. Rather, he chose humility and service as his lifestyle. God selected Joshua because of his heart, not because of his political machinations. The Bible repeatedly mentions Joshua's faithfulness to *all* God's commands (Josh. 5:15; 8:35; 10:40; 11:15, 23; 14:5; 23:6; 24:15, 31).

> **Just as partial obedience is an oxymoron; delayed obedience is also a contradiction in terms.**

There is no such thing as *partial* obedience. Only total obedience satisfies God. Like Joshua, we have the choice—either we will serve God with all our heart or we will be disobedient. Joshua learned that God has His own standard for faithfulness, and that makes our own opinion irrelevant. The writer of Proverbs said, "All the ways of a man are pure in his own eyes, but the Lord weighs the spirits" (Prov. 16:2).

Just as partial obedience is an oxymoron; *delayed* obedience is also a contradiction in terms. To put off doing what God commands is a blatant affront to His sovereignty. The moment God spoke, Joshua knew the next thing he did was crucial. Joshua developed a habit of spontaneous obedience so that when God spoke, Joshua's response was always immediate compliance.

Sometimes Joshua did not know where his obedience would lead him. His ways were not God's ways (Isa. 55:8–9). Nevertheless, he was faithful to God in the small and large assignments. One day he could look back on his life to see a lifelong track record of submission to God.

A faithful life is not built upon good intentions, rededications or New Year's resolutions. It is established on a daily determination to do whatever God says to do. There are no shortcuts to faithfulness. Faithfulness requires a lifetime of daily obedience to the Lord. The accumulation of such obedience defines a mighty servant of God. Joshua became such a person.

SEIZING MOMENTS TO BE FAITHFUL

- Joshua: faithful from the beginning
- Joshua: faithful to his name
- Joshua: a faithful believer
- Joshua: faithful while in the minority
- Joshua: faithful in worship
- Joshua: faithful to God's warnings

QUESTIONS FOR CONSIDERATION

1. How would you characterize the first steps of your walk with God? Were you faithful to do what God asked? How has the way you began your relationship with God affected the way you walk with Him today?

2. What areas of your character have been the most affected since you began following Christ? What areas of your character is God presently working on? How are you cooperating with God as He fashions your character?

3. Are you easily influenced by others? Has your influence on others primarily been for good or for bad?

4. How has God preserved your life? Do you have a sense that God has a purpose for your life? If so, what do you think that might be?

5. Are you satisfied with the way you currently worship God? How do you think God looks at your worship of Him? Do you settle for a shallow spiritual life? When was the last time you had a life-changing encounter with God? What would you need to do to deepen your walk with God?

6. Are there some people around you who serve as reminders of God's judgment? What have you learned by observing how God has dealt with others?

7. Could your life be described as a life of faithfulness?

THREE

GOD BUILDS ON THE PAST

HE WAS BORN INTO HUMBLE CIRCUMSTANCES defined by poverty and hardship. He was a frail and sickly child. As a youth, he longed to serve in the British Royal Navy. He loved the military but he ranked only forty-two out of fifty-eight in his class at the military academy.[1] He was small in stature but he harbored a giant appetite for fame and glory. In fact, his entire life was propelled by this quest for power. He became a force to be reckoned with but his selfish ambitions led Europe into turmoil and warfare for most of his adult life.

Napoleon Bonaparte left an indelible mark on history. According to his biographer, Paul Johnson, Napoleon was responsible for the following developments: history's first large scale military conscription, the rise of German nationalism, the concept of total warfare, the development of the first secret police, large scale professional espionage and the establishment of government propaganda machines. According to Johnson, "The totalitarian state of the twentieth century was the ultimate progeny of the Napoleonic reality and myth."[2]

Furthermore, under Napoleon's leadership, the once mighty nation of France lost 860,000 soldiers and was reduced to a second rate power.[3] What of the man himself? After numerous battles and campaigns, he reached the pinnacle of power, ruling half a continent and eighty million people. Then he plummeted to humiliating defeat and was exiled to a remote island only seven miles wide and nineteen miles long.

Paul Johnson claims that only one man has had more written about him than Napoleon, and that is Jesus Christ. Napoleon's entire life was haunted by his past. His humble birth was shrouded in scandal, which caused world leaders to look down on him with disdain. Despite his brilliant military conquests, the royal families of Europe were reluctant to accept him into their ranks.

Czar Alexander I of Russia forbade Napoleon to marry his daughter, though Napoleon was undoubtedly the most powerful ruler in the world. This rejection may be what ultimately propelled Napoleon to embark on his disastrous invasion of Russia in 1812. Napoleon's numerous insecurities created in him a voracious appetite for recognition. He was an emotional vacuum; nothing could satisfy him—not even a European empire.

It could be argued that hundreds of thousands of Europeans died in one man's vain attempt to achieve satisfaction through the brutal acquisition of power and fame. Ego-driven people become desensitized to the suffering of others. It is acknowledged that few commanders suffered military casualties with greater indifference than Napoleon.

The Duke of Wellington lamented the loss of thousands, but Napoleon boasted he would readily sacrifice a million soldiers to attain his goals. The Duke of Wellington wore his hat with the tips at the front and back so he could easily raise his hat out of courtesy or to return salutes. Napoleon wore his hat squarely on his head—he rarely raised his hat for anyone.[4]

Napoleon could always justify his own ambitious behavior while bitterly condemning the same motives in others. Of his enemies he once complained: "But for them I would have been a man of peace."[5] Such a lifestyle of self-absorption is spiritually deadening. It inevitably leads to isolation. Those who live to satisfy their own ambitions at the expense of others may indeed achieve their goals only to discover that such success is bitter and empty. Like Napoleon, they ultimately live in exile from meaningful relationships and never experience what God intended for them.

Building Blocks

Like Napoleon, Joshua was a military leader who grew up impoverished and suppressed. Yet Joshua's past served as the foundation for his eventual role as God's statesman. Joshua's motives were inverse to Napoleon's. God, not Joshua, set the agenda for Joshua's decisions. God's will, not Joshua's

❦❦❦❦❦❦❦❦❦❦

Joshua's past became the foundation for his eventual role as God's statesman.

❦❦❦❦❦❦❦❦❦❦

ego, galvanized him to action. As a result, every event in Joshua's life became a building block in the magnificent life God was creating.

Joshua's life was not dependent on random chance or the exertion of human will. His was a purposeful life that brought glory to God. Joshua was not a prisoner of his past; he overcame his upbringing and allowed God to build for him a bright future.

In this chapter we will examine how the past affects our leadership ability and our leadership possibilities. Joshua's life and leadership experience raise several relevant issues for us.

How does our past affect our leadership ability? For example, some people grew up in dysfunctional homes devoid of parental nurture. As a result, they lack self-confidence and certain people skills essential for strong leadership. Has their past precluded them from any hope of leading in the future?

Is the way we follow today important in determining whether or not we lead tomorrow? Also, are all people called to lead at some level? Is the reason certain people always remain in an assistant's role because they stopped allowing God to develop them into the leaders they could have become if they had only yielded to His will? Or, is it a legitimate calling to be an assistant all your life?

How do we follow a great leader? How do we build upon what has gone before us?

What difference does the Holy Spirit make in our leadership? Can the Spirit make anyone into a leader? How is the working of the Holy Spirit in our lives a prerequisite for God's future assignments for us?

How do leaders cope with change? The organization as they first knew it may have changed significantly. The circumstances in which they work may be in flux. How do leaders continue to lead their people forward when those things they counted on in the past are no longer a reality? These are the practical issues today's leaders must address. Studying how Joshua dealt with them will shed light on our circumstances as well.

This chapter will examine Joshua's life from the context of his past. At least two types of history exercise a significant influence upon people. The first is that over which you have no control: the nationality of your birth, your family's socioeconomic status, the presence or absence of a nurturing atmosphere in your home, and so on.

Likewise, the history of the organization you lead is something you inherit: the church you serve was torn by a split five years before you arrived as pastor; your predecessor in the company embezzled funds from the business and now you work under a cloud of suspicion. This history occurred completely apart from you but now bears its weight upon you.

A second type of history is your own personal background. The way you conducted your life as a young person can directly impact your later adult life. The diligence with which you pursued your education or your first jobs can exact long-lasting consequences. This is the more recent history in your life and it includes events and attitudes over which you exercised some control. You are now facing the consequences for an accumulation of decisions you made in earlier years.

Both Joshua's national history and his personal history profoundly affected the role he played as a spiritual leader. Every day Joshua faced the consequences of mistakes others had committed. He also reaped the benefit of the wise decisions he had made in his past. Let us consider some of the significant ways history intersected Joshua's life.

JOSHUA WAS FIRST A GOOD ASSISTANT

The Duke of Wellington was bewildered by the concept of "second in commands." He saw no use for them, since everyone was expected to follow the orders of the first in command. The Duke only desired subordinates.[6] Yet one of the main reasons Joshua became such a successful leader was because he first was a faithful and conscientious assistant.

There is no such thing as a born leader. Becoming a good leader is a process. When God prepares someone for a significant assignment, he is thorough and systematic. His pattern, as revealed in the Scriptures, is to build character and leadership skills step by step. When people prove faithful in small assignments, they are given larger ones (Matt. 25:21, 23).

> There is no such thing as a born leader. Becoming a good leader is a process.

Generally when God wants to develop leaders He begins by teaching them how to be good followers. However, not everyone is comfortable with secondary positions. Often aspiring leaders chafe under their subordinant roles in their impatience to take charge. But both biblical and secular history relates numerous examples of successful leaders who first proved themselves faithful followers.

Jacob's son Joseph seemed to know this instinctively as he faithfully served Potiphar and the Egyptian jailor before reaching the apex of power under the Pharaoh. Conversely, the disciple Peter had to go against his impulsive, outspoken nature to learn this truth.

Dwight Eisenhower was an outstanding assistant. In fact, his effectiveness as an aide kept him out of military action during World War One (a fact that troubled him greatly). Eisenhower served under General Douglas MacArthur and General George Marshall, the two most renowned American generals of that day. Eisenhower's organizational ability was so exceptional that neither general was willing to release him to serve in active combat.

Eisenhower claimed his ambition in the army "was to make everybody I worked for regretful when I was ordered to other duty."[7] But the old adage of the cream rising to the top proved true, and Eisenhower's dedication to serving his superiors ultimately led him to one of the most exalted positions in American military history. He eventually served as one of America's most popular presidents.

Joshua had the mettle required to serve as a capable assistant before taking over command himself. Moses was not the easiest person to assist. He was poor at delegation (Ex. 18:13–27). He could not always handle those with opposing opinions (Num. 13:28–14:5). He was susceptible to outbursts of anger (Ex. 2:11–12; 32:19; Num. 20:10–11). Nonetheless, there is no record of Joshua complaining about Moses. On the contrary, he repeatedly defended his leader's honor and reputation.

While he served as Moses' assistant, Joshua was protective of his leader's position and authority among the people. When Eldad and Medad began prophesying in the camp, Joshua saw this as a challenge to Moses' leadership, so he urged Moses to stop them (Num. 11:28).

Joshua never appears concerned about building his reputation or gaining recognition for his accomplishments.

But Moses, with characteristic humility, gently and wisely responded, "Are you zealous for my sake? Oh, that all the LORD'S people were prophets and that the LORD would put His Spirit upon them!" (Num. 11:29). Joshua never sided with Moses' critics, of whom there were many. Rather, Joshua's loyalty lay with his leader and he would support him even in the face of widespread unpopularity.

Joshua never appeared concerned with building his own reputation or gaining recognition for his own accomplishments. He simply served to the best of his ability wherever God placed him. It was God who determined how and when Joshua was promoted as a leader and it was God who ultimately chose to make Joshua one of the most successful and famous generals in his nation's history.

In one of American history's ironies, John Adams faced the double challenge of being a loyal associate and working with a disloyal one. Perhaps Adams's two greatest achievements came not from his own accomplishments but from the accomplishments of those he nominated. At the crucial outset of the American Revolution, Adams nominated George Washington to command the revolutionary army. He also nominated Thomas Jefferson to draft the Declaration of Independence.

Chosen himself in 1788 as the first vice president of the United States and serving under the venerable George Washington, Adams had to define for posterity what an American vice president was to do, which was very little. Washington rarely consulted with him or publicly praised him. Yet Adams accepted his role as second to Washington and diligently fulfilled his responsibilities. During his eight years as vice president, Adams cast thirty-one tie-breaking votes in the Senate, all in favor of Washington's administration.

After two terms, Washington retired and Adams was elected president in 1796. Thomas Jefferson was his vice president. Adams viewed Jefferson as a friend; they had spent many pleasant days together in diplomatic service in France and England. Yet they had developed radically divergent political views.

Adams was a Federalist, seeking to strengthen the union that bound the fledgling nation together. Jefferson was a Republican, defending the rights of individuals and states against the intrusion of centralizing, federalist powers. While Adams sought to rise above party politics and to govern in the best interests of America, Jefferson covertly led the emerging Republican Party in ever intensifying attacks upon the government and against Adams. Jefferson was actively undermining the government to the point of financing James Callender, who published vicious, libelous attacks against Adams.

In the only case of an American vice president running against the president, Jefferson defeated Adams in the 1800 election. It would take decades before the two former friends were reconciled. Ironically, because of a loophole in the Constitution at that time, Jefferson and his running mate, Aaron Burr, received the identical number of electoral votes, creating confusion over who was to be president and who would be vice president. Even though Jefferson had been the presidential candidate, Burr refused to defer to him, leading to numerous votes in the House of Representatives before Jefferson won the presidency. Obviously Jefferson was already reaping what he had sown!

The difference between the top position and the second in command can be enormous. While there can be far more prestige and recognition coming to the former, there are also burdens they carry that no one else can share. Joshua would have certainly seen some advantages to remaining second in command.

Leading an entire nation, especially one as recalcitrant as Israel, would have been an onerous burden to assume. People lined up for hours to speak with Moses, not Joshua. Malcontents castigated Moses, not Joshua. Joshua saw firsthand how unappreciated Moses often was for his efforts.

Joshua could have settled into a comfortable position in middle management and closed the door to what God had in mind for him. Joshua could have ended his days as Moses' assistant and history would have granted him minor mention in the Scriptural record, but he would have robbed himself and his country of the mighty work God intended to do through his life.

A Question About Assistant Roles

This raises an important issue. Would Joshua have been just as success-ful had he always remained Moses' assistant? Can the role of assistant be a legitimate calling in itself or is it merely a step in God's preparation process for a higher leadership position? If people are continually growing and developing in their leadership skills, will they not eventually be prepared to assume a senior leadership role? These are questions those in secondary lead-ership roles must ask.

Not everyone who serves in middle management is necessarily called to upper management. Their posi-tion in their organization does not reflect whether or not God is working in their lives. Personal and pro-fessional development can and does take place at any level of an organization. Leadership is not performed exclusively at the top of the organizational chart.

The key is not our aspirations or our ego needs or our insecurities. The key is God's assignment.

We know numerous associate pastors and middle managers who are at the center of all that is happening in their organizations. One does not have to spend much time around them to rec-ognize God is using them powerfully in the roles to which He has called them. They experience challenges and contentment where they are and they do not require promotions to be effective.

The key to one's leadership position rests with God. God assigns some people to work as assistants to other leaders. God calls others into roles as senior leaders.

The key is not our aspirations or our ego needs or our insecurities. The key is God's assignment. Those coveting positions of top leadership may not pos-sess the character to hold such a position. On the other hand, some people avoiding leadership positions may be running from God's will. Every one of us must stand before God and ask what God is calling us to do, regardless of our preferences.

❦❦❦❦❦❦❦❦❦❦❦

**Joshua sought
to grow personally
in whatever
position God
assigned to him.**

❦❦❦❦❦❦❦❦❦❦❦

Many talented people avoid leadership positions like the plague! Others do not feel called by God to lead. Some are fearful to lead. Many suffer insecurities that convince them they cannot lead. Some recognize that to lead would require the investment of far more effort than they are willing to make. Others possess a profound sense of humility that prefers to support others who are in the forefront. Not everyone is attracted to top leadership positions. Those who believe a supportive role is their calling can learn at least three significant lessons from Joshua:

Lesson 1: Joshua always sought to grow personally in whatever position God assigned to him. He didn't confine himself to his own comfort level. He grew personally and professionally throughout his life. Each step of faith was foundational for greater accomplishments God purposed to complete through him. Not all of God's greater assignments for Joshua resulted in a promotion or a new leadership position. But every new challenge revealed a little more to Joshua about who God is. It is often through crises a leader experiences the deepest dimensions of God's love and power. God is always seeking to work in the lives of His servants to increase their trust in Him (Matt. 25:14–30; Luke 19:17).

Forty years is a long time to wait for a promotion. But for Joshua, those four decades were anything but stagnant. He walked through numerous diverse and multifaceted challenges during his time in the desert. God taught Joshua the key to people's success is not the rung they reach on the corporate ladder but the level of intimacy they reach with God. Whether Joshua was experiencing prosperity in the promised land or suffering exile in the wilderness, he could still enjoy a close relationship with almighty God.

The position Joshua held had nothing to do with his accessibility to God. When Joshua's lengthy stint as Moses' assistant drew to a close, he emerged fully prepared to lead because of all God had been doing in his life. When Joshua became the senior leader of the Israelites, it was not to escape

the monotony or emptiness of his role as an assistant; it was a natural step in the process of walking
with God year by year.

> **God's assignments do not always coincide with career advancement.**

That being said, whether it is short term or long
term, the job of assistant requires a clear sense of
calling. Joshua knew he was called to an associate's
role. Whether or not God ever adjusted that role
was up to God. Joshua's responsibility was to serve. Likewise, a person ought
to remain in his secondary leadership role for as long as he continues to feel
a specific calling to it.

Lesson 2: Christians who experience success as assistants keep their focus on
the kingdom of God rather than on their careers. We've known many people
who were so active in their local churches that they bypassed promotions and
transfers in their jobs, along with the accompanying salaries and prestige.
They did so because the new role would have hindered them from serving the
Lord in the same manner they were accustomed to in their current position.

Some business people, knowing they were called first to be leaders in
their own homes, have declined promotions because the increased responsibilities would create undue hardships on their families. Such people clearly
understand the difference between their vocation and their calling.
Whereas they must have a vocation to earn a living, their calling is to bring
glory to God. God's assignments do not always coincide with career
advancement. Although they may never reach the apex of power in their
organization, they will be used mightily to extend God's kingdom. One's
calling should always take precedence over one's career.

Lesson 3: Joshua modeled a deep-rooted humility. There is no evidence Joshua
struggled with ego. He never made demands on Moses or the people for recognition of his service. He did not submit a résumé for the position Moses was
vacating. He wholly trusted his career into the sovereign hands of God.

Humble people like Joshua find joy in serving and do not need the
limelight to find contentment. These people derive pleasure from making

others successful. History's great leaders have invariably been surrounded with such people. Successful generals such as Dwight Eisenhower had capable associates such as Omar Bradley and George Patton willingly serving under him.

One of the primary reasons for the heralded success of Queen Elizabeth I was her chief counselor, Sir William Cecil. He served her with devotion and efficiency for most of his adult life. Their relationship has been described as "one of the most remarkable relationships in English history."[8]

Even when he was elderly and dying, his queen could not do without him: "Now seventy-eight, he was white-haired and shrunken, but still in harness because the queen, having relied on him for over half a century, would not let him resign, even though she knew he was deaf, in constant pain with gout, and could barely hold a pen."[9] As Cecil languished, the famous monarch spoon-fed him his meals and cared for him until his death. Such was her indebtedness to her loyal servant.

One of the great partnerships in American military history occurred between General Robert E. Lee and General Stonewall Jackson. Of Jackson, Lee claimed: "I had such implicit confidence in Jackson's skill and energy that I never troubled myself to give him detailed instructions. The most general suggestions were all that he needed."[10]

When critics charged that Jackson was the one responsible for the Confederate victories and that Lee was too cautious, Jackson retorted: "He is cautious. He ought to be. But he is *not* slow. Lee is a phenomenon. He is the only man whom I would follow blindfold."[11]

When Jackson was mortally wounded after his brilliant victory at the Battle of Chancellorsville, Lee quickly wrote to him and said, "Could I have directed events, I should have chosen for the good of the country to have been disabled in your stead." Jackson's response was "Better that ten Jacksons should fall than one Lee."

When it appeared that Jackson was recovering, Lee playfully wrote to his fallen lieutenant, "You are better off than I am, for while you have only lost your *left*, I have lost my *right* arm."[12] Few, if any, outstanding leaders achieve success without the dedicated service of capable associates.

A caution is in order here. While God calls some people to invest themselves in supportive roles all their lives, others grasp these positions in default of what God intended for them. Associates who remain in their roles because they are unwilling to assume more responsibility, will never experience the same level of fulfillment as people who are associates because that is exactly where God called them to be.

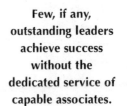

Few, if any, outstanding leaders achieve success without the dedicated service of capable associates.

Again, the key is God's will. Every Christian would do well to learn from Joshua's example. He was content in his role as an associate, but he was also willing to take on the role of primary leader if God told him to do so. Spiritual leaders maintain an obedient attitude. They find fulfillment in whatever role God assigns them, but this does not mean they close themselves off to whatever new direction God has for them. If you are currently in an associate position, it's crucial for you to clarify whether you are there at God's invitation or at your own hesitation.

JOSHUA SUCCEEDED A GREAT LEADER

Replacing a successful leader is a good thing. But stepping into the shoes of a great leader puts the newcomer at a distinct disadvantage. The issue is expectations. Those accustomed to highly effective leadership expect nothing less from the successor. Leadership styles differ, and most people can eventually adjust to that, but there are higher expectations when the predecessor set the bar high. This can certainly intimidate novice leaders who have not yet reached their full potential. How would you like to have followed the man Joshua succeeded? Scripture describes Moses at the end of his life this way:

> But since then there has not arisen in Israel a prophet like Moses, whom the LORD knew face to face, in all the signs and wonders which the LORD sent him to do in the land of Egypt, before Pharaoh, before all his servants, and in all his land, and by all that mighty power and all the great terror which Moses performed in the sight of all Israel. (Deuteronomy 34:10–12)

**You can tell a lot
about leaders
by watching how
they handle the
ghosts of
their predecessors.**

There could be no questioning Moses' stellar track record. He set an incredibly high standard. When a sea blocked the way, Moses parted it! When his countrymen were hungry, he showered them with manna and quail from the sky! When they were thirsty, he called forth water from a rock! After he spoke with God, his face took on a supernatural glow! Those who criticized him contracted leprosy! (Num. 12:1–16). Those who opposed him saw the earth open up to swallow them in its depths! (Num. 16:28–35). God poured out His power through Moses' life in an unprecedented way. Now Moses was gone and the people looked to Joshua to see what kind of leader *he* would be.

Throughout the book of Joshua, Moses is called "the servant of the Lord" (Josh. 1:1; 8:31; 9:24; 12:6). Joshua, on the other hand, is described as "Moses' servant" (Ex. 24:13; 33:11; Num. 11:28; Josh. 1:1). The Bible does not call Joshua the "servant of the Lord" until his death (Josh. 24:29; Judg. 2:8). What was it like for Joshua to be known as "the servant of Moses"? After all, Joshua was a mighty warrior in his own right. He had been faithful to God in all things, even more so than Moses had been. It may have seemed that Joshua would always remain eclipsed in Moses' shadow.

It is one thing to serve *under* a great leader; it is another thing to *succeed* a great leader. How hard is it to follow an excellent leader? Historians generally agree that whatever president followed the revered George Washington was doomed to failure. John Adams's own impeccable credentials did not save him from inevitable and numerous comparisons to the victorious general of the Revolutionary War.

Richard Nixon loathed John F. Kennedy and all he represented. A wealthy, handsome, charismatic aristocrat, Kennedy was everything Nixon was not. During one election campaign Nixon was told by a tactless well-wisher that it was too bad he couldn't do anything about his face![13] Throughout Nixon's presidency he was haunted by the specter of the man who had defeated him for president and captured the hearts and imaginations of Americans in a way Nixon was unable to do.

You can tell a lot about leaders by watching how they handle the ghosts of their predecessors. Consider the new pastor who immediately removes all pictures and reminders of the former pastor from view. Then he systematically dismantles any initiative begun by his predecessor so that he can fashion the church into *his* image. He may justify his actions as "strong leadership" or "taking the church in a new direction." But is it insecurity that makes him reluctant to build upon what God accomplished in the past rather than tearing it down and starting over?

We know one new pastor who decided to relocate his church from its extensive property because the facilities reminded him and the people of a former pastor! We have also known misguided pastors whose entire "ministries" seemed centered on demolishing what beloved former pastors had painstakingly accomplished.

THE HURDLE OF PRIDE

The greatest obstacle in effectively succeeding an esteemed leader is the hurdle of pride. Joshua did not seem to resent following the mighty Moses, though he must have felt daunted by the task. Perhaps that's why, when Joshua first assumed command, God repeatedly encouraged him not to be afraid but to be courageous (Josh. 1:6–7, 9).

Joshua accepted Moses' work as foundational to his own rather than as a threat to his success. Joshua did not have to dismantle or criticize Moses' accomplishments in order to elevate himself; instead he chose to build upon the foundation Moses had laid. That is why God honored him. Joshua honored God by honoring what God had done through Moses.

The same situation was later mirrored in the relationship between the prophet Elijah and his protégé, Elisha. Elijah was one of the greatest prophets in history. He prayed and the rain stopped falling for three years. His prayers also brought fire descending from heaven to consume his sacrifice, altar and all (1 Kings 18:20–46). What an intimidating leader to replace!

The greatest obstacle in effectively succeeding an esteemed leader is the hurdle of pride.

Faithfulness comes from your character, not from your title.

When Elisha learned he would be Elijah's successor, he asked for and received a "double portion" of the Spirit that inhabited Elijah. Elisha knew it was God's Spirit who empowered Elijah and the same Spirit would have to strengthen him if he were to follow such a famous prophet.

Bible scholars identify eight miracles performed by Elijah and sixteen by Elisha. Elisha didn't resent God's activity in his predecessor's life. Neither did he feel threatened by Elijah's illustrious career. He learned from it. He wisely concluded if God's Spirit worked so powerfully through Elijah, the same Spirit could empower him for a dynamic ministry as well.

The apostle Paul addressed this issue with the church at Corinth. Some of the Corinthian believers had been deeply affected by Apollos's ministry. Others were staunchly loyal to Paul. To Paul's dismay, the church was dividing according to which spiritual leader held their allegiance. Paul clarified: "I planted, Apollos watered, but God gave the increase" (1 Cor. 3:6).

God's servants come and go, but God is the one who accomplishes the work. Spiritual leaders have a role to play but they are instruments in God's hand. Leaders are wise to remember that long after they leave their organization, God will remain. And, as long as they are in their leadership positions, they are God's servants. Pride has no place in service to God.

JOSHUA'S PAST PREPARED HIM FOR THE FUTURE

We once knew a young man who longed to be the outreach director for his church's Sunday School program. He was sincere, and confident he could do a good job. The problem was that he did not attend Sunday School himself. When this was pointed out to him, he quickly rejoined that he *would* attend if he were given the position! He would be his own first recruit! While his enthusiasm was commendable, this fellow misguidedly assumed a leadership position would automatically make him something he was not. Of course this is not true. Faithfulness comes from your character, not from your title.

Joshua did not become a person of integrity *after* his appointment as

leader. His integrity preceded and led to his assign-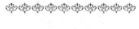
ment. Did Joshua become a man of God the
moment Moses laid hands on him? No. The Bible
reveals that when Moses commissioned him, Joshua
was already filled with the Holy Spirit: "And the
LORD said to Moses: "Take Joshua the son of Nun
with you, a man in whom is the Spirit, and lay your
hand on him; set him before Eleazar the priest and
before all the congregation, and inaugurate him in
their sight" (Num. 27:18–19).

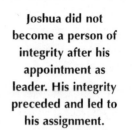

> Joshua did not
> become a person of
> integrity after his
> appointment as
> leader. His integrity
> preceded and led to
> his assignment.

Moses apparently laid his hands on Joshua because the Spirit was *already* working powerfully in Joshua. How did Moses know who his successor would be? God showed him the man in whom His Spirit had already been powerfully working. Moses simply affirmed the Holy Spirit's presence in Joshua's life.

Can you picture God saying, "Lay your hands on Joshua and when he realizes I have called him, he will get more serious about his faith?" Joshua already *was* a Spirit-filled man of God. That is why God chose him for such a significant assignment. During Old Testament times, God gave people tasks and then enabled them to accomplish their assignment by placing the Holy Spirit in their lives.

For example, God called Bezalel to construct the tabernacle and then "filled him with the Spirit of God, in wisdom, in understanding, in knowledge, and in all manner of workmanship" (Ex. 31:1–3). God commissioned Samson as a deliverer for his people and then placed his Spirit on him to give him unusual strength (Judg. 14:19; 15:14). In Joshua's case the gift of the Spirit came *before* the assignment, a truly unusual occurrence for the Old Testament era.

Joshua's new assignment was a natural outflow of what God had already been doing in his life. God did not begin working in Joshua's life once he became a leader. Rather, Joshua became the leader *because* God had already been working in his life. Your relationship with God is far more important than any position. Those who hold a position of spiritual leadership without experiencing the active working of the Holy Spirit are courting humiliating failure.

If you are a spiritual leader, or if you want to become one, the most important thing you can do is to concentrate on your walk with God. If the Holy Spirit is actively involved in your life, guiding your decisions and empowering your actions, then your life will exert a tremendous influence on others.

Those who hold a position of spiritual leadership without experiencing the active working of the Holy Spirit are courting humiliating failure.

When Joshua took over from Moses, he inherited some logistical headaches. One of his most pressing concerns was how to feed the vast multitude under his care. Moses had committed his grievous sin while attempting to provide water for the vast crowd (Num. 20:1–13). For forty years the Israelites had gathered manna every morning to feed their families for that day. It was like a light frost on the ground that tasted like milk and honey (Ex. 16:14, 31). Thus they were reminded daily of what they were missing in the promised land. It was only a faint taste of what they would have enjoyed in abundance, had they obeyed God.

Then an interesting thing happened once Joshua led the Israelites across the Jordan River into the promised land. The manna that had routinely fallen from heaven for forty years suddenly stopped (Josh. 5:12). Manna was all the young Israelites knew. They had been gathering it each morning for their entire lives. It met their needs nutritionally but they had never tasted "real" food. Then suddenly the manna ceased.

Now that they were in the luxuriant promised land, the Israelites needn't continue their subsistence lifestyle. God wanted them to enjoy the bounty He had provided them, even if it meant taking it away from giants in walled cities! This posed a problem for Joshua. Food no longer fell from the sky; now they had to fight for it. Moses had his concerns in the wilderness and now, in the promised land, Joshua had his own unique challenges.

Leaders do not choose the time in which they lead. Some serve in periods of prosperity and peace. Others come to the helm just as their ship enters turbulent waters. Dwight Eisenhower was president during the prosperous 1950s when the United States was the leading world superpower, enjoying dominance in nuclear firepower.

Conversely, Lyndon Johnson inherited a government recoiling from the assassination of its popular president, embroiled in the Vietnam conflict and facing a formidable rival superpower. Abraham Lincoln came to the American presidency at the brink of the most disastrous war in his nation's history. During the presidential election, the southern states did not even carry his name on the ballots. When he was elected, he was burned in effigy in the South.

Sometimes, adversity actually propels leaders to greatness by drawing on the deep reserves of their character. Despite the horrendous conditions Lincoln encountered as the new chief executive, he resolutely rose to the challenges and became what many historians consider the greatest president in American history. Leaders do not complain about the unique challenges facing them. True leaders tackle challenges and, with God's help, overcome them.

> **Leaders do not complain about the unique challenges facing them. True leaders tackle challenges and, with God's help, overcome them.**

Some people struggle with change. They like to "nestle in" to an organization and keep everything the way it is. Yet change is occurring today at a dizzying pace. Those who get lost in the sentimental memories of yesterday will be of no use to organizations today.

Modern leaders accept change, whether good or bad, as a matter of course. Rather than resisting change, they capitalize on it. Rather than grieving over what has been lost, they grow excited about what can become. Astute leaders embrace the reality of inevitable change and they seek ways God will use them to make a significant difference in the midst of it.

Joshua had the privilege of leading his people into a lush and fertile land. But along with this opportunity came a completely new set of demands. Whereas Moses hadn't had to concern himself with feeding his people for forty years, Joshua was going to face this enormous challenge daily. It was a significant additional burden for Joshua.

However, rather than bemoaning this fact, Joshua faced the future boldly, based on his observations from the past. The lesson Joshua learned while serving under Moses was not that God provided *manna* but that God *provided.* God had sustained the Israelites for forty years, even while they were disobedient. Surely they could trust God's care as they obeyed Him in the present.

The lesson Joshua learned while serving under Moses was not that God provided manna but that God provided.

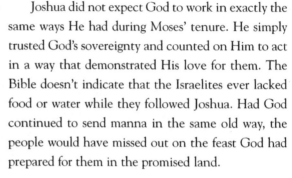

Joshua did not expect God to work in exactly the same ways He had during Moses' tenure. He simply trusted God's sovereignty and counted on Him to act in a way that demonstrated His love for them. The Bible doesn't indicate that the Israelites ever lacked food or water while they followed Joshua. Had God continued to send manna in the same old way, the people would have missed out on the feast God had prepared for them in the promised land.

CONCLUSION

Joshua's difficult beginnings could have crippled him with insecurities. But Joshua didn't focus on his past, except to learn from it. He allowed God to create something unique with his life. Joshua trusted God to guide him through each new situation.

As Moses' assistant, Joshua was diligent and patient. He allowed God to work thoroughly in his life. Joshua didn't campaign for a prominent position among the Israelites. He simply served God and trusted Him. God is the one who chose Joshua and fashioned him into an effective and respected leader.

Now it's time for some honest self-evaluation. First, consider the type of follower you are. Everyone is accountable to someone. Are you loyal? Dependable? Are you the type of follower you would like to have serving under you?

Second, consider what type of leader you are. Are you a dynamic person who is always learning and growing? Or, have you settled into an attitude of complacency? Leaders, of all people, can never afford to stop growing.

If God has been stretching you through your circumstances, how are you facing the challenge? Could He be preparing you for a new role? What do you value more—your relationship with God or your position with people?

GOD BUILDS ON THE PAST

- Joshua was first a good assistant.
- Joshua succeeded a great leader.
- Joshua's past prepared him for the future.

QUESTIONS FOR CONSIDERATION

1. Would you want someone to serve under you in the same manner you work under your leader? Why or why not?

2. Have you mastered the art of being a good follower? What characteristics have you demonstrated as a follower that would indicate you could be a good leader?

3. Have you grown complacent in your present position? What truths has God been teaching you? Do you sense He might be preparing you for something new?

4. How does the history of your walk with God help you face today's challenges? Do you resent the difficult circumstances in your life right now? What might God be seeking to teach you through them?

5. Do you value your relationship with God more highly than your position with people? What is the evidence?

FOUR

GOD'S PRESENCE:
THE SECRET TO SUCCESS

HE'D BEEN A RESPECTED MINISTER for seventeen years. Week after week he reverently led worship services, preached relevant sermons, and administered the church ordinances. He'd performed dozens of weddings and funerals. Still, a nagging sense of uneasiness tugged at his soul. He sensed there ought to be more spiritual power in his ministry.

He later claimed: "Oh, the deceit of the human heart! I knew how unfit I was, Oh, I would question my salvation, because I tried to live consistently. But I knew barrenness . . . barrenness in my spirit."[1] As time passed his discomfort intensified. Finally, in desperation, he announced to his concerned family: "I'm going to my study and I want you to leave me alone. I'm going to seek a meeting with God."

He cloistered himself in his study and committed to pray until God freed him. At one point his sixteen-year-old daughter pled with her father, "Daddy, whatever it costs, go through with God." After spending several hours before the Lord, the desperate pastor experienced a profound, life-changing encounter with God early in the dawn.

Later, he claimed: "After spending seventeen years in a barren wilderness, baffled and frustrated in Christian work and witness, I suddenly came to realize that God had made provision for clean hands and a pure heart. And on my face in my own study at five o'clock in the morning I came to know the recovering power of the blood of Christ . . ."[2]

Duncan Campbell had been renewed. Immediately, others began experiencing revival as well. Campbell preached in meetings across Scotland. Everywhere he went, God's power was manifested. In 1949 he was invited to conduct a ten-day series of revival services at Barvas on the Isle of Lewis. After his first message, it seemed as if nothing extraordinary had occurred. As he prepared to leave, however, the Spirit suddenly descended upon the congregation. To Campbell's surprise he discovered several hundred people gathered outside the church doors. They had arrived from all over the region, with no sense of why they had come except they felt compelled to do so.

As the weeks passed, more and more unusual events took place. Four hundred people gathered at the police station during the early morning hours and Campbell preached to them. After one service, he passed people kneeling by the roadside overcome with conviction of their sin, crying out to God for forgiveness.

One evening he was made aware that a large crowd had spontaneously assembled in a large field. There were too many people to fit in the church so they gathered outdoors. Campbell preached to them and many were converted. The revival swept across the Hebrides Islands for several years.[3]

Twenty years later, the elderly Campbell was in Saskatoon, Canada, preaching at Ebenezer Baptist Church. He declared his belief that revival was coming to western Canada and it would begin at that church. Within two years the revival he foretold had come.

God chose to fill Duncan Campbell with spiritual power. After his life-changing encounter with God, his preaching took on new life. Even when he delivered sermons he had preached before, there was a significant difference. Campbell observed: "I went out to preach the same sermons that I'd been preaching for seventeen years . . . with this difference—that I saw hundreds converted, hundreds brought savingly to Christ."[4]

The Holy Spirit anointed his ministry and God used him powerfully. The key was not in Campbell's preaching skills but in God's powerful presence. The difference the Holy Spirit makes in a life is astronomical. No one, no matter how creative or

He needed more than strategic planning to accomplish God's purposes. He needed God.

talented, can duplicate or manufacture what the Spirit can do in the life of someone yielded to God.

Joshua was a skilled military leader but his success came from his walk with God, not from his military prowess. He needed more than strategic planning to accomplish God's purposes. He needed God. This chapter will examine some of the ways God's presence made a pronounced difference in Joshua's leading.

JOSHUA EXERCISED GOOD LEADERSHIP

The ability and willingness to take decisive and timely action can mean the difference between victory and defeat.

Clearly Joshua's success was rooted in his dependence on God. Yet Joshua also modeled good leadership principles as he led the Israelites. For example, Joshua knew how to act quickly. The ability and willingness to take decisive and timely action can mean the difference between victory and defeat. Joshua used the rapid advance of his army to throw his enemies off balance.

When Israel's allies, the Gibeonites, were suddenly besieged by five Amorite kings, it appeared the Amorites could easily overwhelm the vastly outnumbered Gibeonites (Josh. 10:9). Joshua responded immediately and marched his men from Gilgal through the night. The Israelites surprised the Amorites the following morning, catching them off guard and winning a spectacular victory.

Joshua worked closely with his key leaders. The elders of Israel apparently respected him. Unlike Moses who tended at times to work alone (Ex. 18:1–27; 33:7), Joshua was a team player. Joshua was secure in his walk with God. He never appeared intimidated or threatened by other influential leaders. The people did not complain or rebel against his leadership. In fact, they continued to follow his instructions even after his death until their generation passed from the scene (Judg. 2:7).

Modern leadership gurus regularly advocate "servant leadership" as the preeminent way to influence others. In that regard, Joshua was centuries ahead of his time. He refused to set himself above the hardships his people experienced. He was God's servant, not the people's king, and that reality dramatically influenced the way he led people. When he set an ambush for the people of Ai, he personally took the place of greatest peril. He intentionally occupied the most dangerous position on the battlefield (Josh. 8:4–22).

Joshua could have hidden in ambush with twenty-five thousand men; instead he stationed himself among the five thousand soldiers who staged a difficult retreat so the enemy would chase after them and abandon the protection of their city. Such courageous leadership did not go unnoticed among his men. Soldiers are much more motivated to follow a leader who never asks them to do anything he is not willing to do himself.

LESSONS FROM HISTORY

Some of history's most famous military leaders refused to order their people to do something they, themselves, were reluctant to do. George Washington seemed impervious to enemy bullets despite the fact that his coat and hat would be riddled with holes after combat. It was Washington who mused: "I heard the bullets whistle, and believe me there is something charming in the sound."[5]

Napoleon Bonaparte had at least nineteen horses shot out from under him while he led his troops in battle! The fierce fighting in which he engaged left him a face wound and a bayonet wound in the thigh.

When the enemy Gauls began to overrun his Roman legions, Caesar rushed to the front lines, calling his centurions by name to follow him. Caesar's biographer notes: "Despite his far from robust constitution, he shared in all their dangers, exertions and privations."[6]

It has been said that no Greek soldier suffered more wounds than their general, Alexander the Great. He often accompanied his soldiers into the most dangerous situations. When he led his men through a barren desert, he refused to eat or drink any more than they did. One well-wisher gave him a flask of water, but he poured it out on the ground, refusing to accept more sustenance than his lowest ranking men received.[7]

Horatio Nelson was the much-loved commander of the British fleet. Nelson often remained in an exposed position during the fiercest battles.

❧❧❧❧❧❧❧❧❧❧

Some of history's most famous military leaders refused to order their people to do something they, themselves, were unwilling to do.

❧❧❧❧❧❧❧❧❧❧

During one attack he was the second man to board an enemy ship. Due to such heroic leadership, Nelson lost an eye, his teeth, and an arm, and suffered numerous other wounds during his battles. Not surprisingly, Nelson's men gladly followed him anywhere.

Over the course of the American Civil War, there were numerous occasions for brave leadership on both sides. During the battle for Fort Donelson, General Grant turned to General C. F. Smith and said, "General Smith . . . all has failed to our right. You must take Fort Donelson." "I will do it," General Smith replied.

Smith returned to his troops and prepared them to charge against an entrenched enemy without firing a shot. He placed the Second Iowa Regiment at the front and exclaimed, "Second Iowa, you must take the fort. I will lead you." With that, the veteran general sat high on his horse and fearlessly led his men into the withering enemy fire.

When his brave troops recoiled under the intense enemy fusillade, Smith yelled, "No flinching now, my lads, this is the way. Come on." One of his soldiers later confessed, "I was nearly scared to death . . . but I saw the Old Man's white mustache over his shoulder, and I went on."[8] Smith's soldiers were victorious and the fort was eventually surrendered.

A highly respected leader himself, Joshua did not use his prominent position for selfish purposes. After having faithfully led the Israelites to a brilliant conquest of Canaan, we do not find Joshua ever making demands of his people as a reward for his services. We never hear of an exalted title or extravagant wealth that came to Joshua as a prize for his success.

American military leaders such as George Washington, Ulysses Grant, Theodore Roosevelt, and Dwight Eisenhower brokered their military success to later achieve the presidency. Arthur Wesley never lost a battle for Britain; he was made the Duke of Wellington. John Churchill, likewise undefeated, became the Duke of Marlborough; Queen Ann built a magnificent estate for him at Blenheim as a monument to his epic victory over their enemies. While serving their nation brilliantly, all these men were rewarded handsomely.

We never see Joshua demanding respect from his people. There are no accusations of mismanagement of funds or of abuse of power. The Israelites believed Joshua was leading in order to bring glory to God and to bless the people of God. Such leadership inspired a loyal following. Jesus explained this leadership approach:

> You know that the rulers of the Gentiles lord it over them, and those who are great exercise authority over them. Yet it shall not be so among you; but whoever desires to become great among you, let him be your servant. And whoever desires to be first among you, let him be your slave—just as the Son of Man did not come to be served, but to serve, and to give His life a ransom for many. (Matthew 20:25–28)

Joshua can take his rightful place as a fearless military leader in his own right. He seems to have been a natural leader in many respects. Yet Joshua had something these other leaders lacked: he had God's presence. George Washington was courageous, but he lost more battles than he won. Admiral Nelson was fearless, but he had the world's greatest navy at

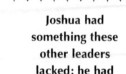

Joshua had something these other leaders lacked: he had God's presence.

his disposal. Likewise, Alexander the Great and Julius Caesar had the best troops in the world available to them. Joshua, however, had a defeated, ragtag group of former slaves and, with God's guidance, he achieved seemingly impossible victories. That took more than good leadership; it took God's presence.

JOSHUA RECEIVED GOD'S AFFIRMATION

Joshua inherited a monumental assignment from Moses. He was expected to succeed where his mentor had failed. He knew the people had grumbled against Moses for forty years; he probably expected his stubborn countrymen to resist his leadership as well. God's words must have brought tremendous relief to Joshua as he prepared to lead the Israelites. This is what the Lord told him:

No man shall be able to stand before you all the days of your life; as I was with Moses, so I will be with you. I will not leave you nor forsake you. Be strong and of good courage, for to this people you shall divide as an inheritance the land which I swore to their fathers to give them. Only be strong and very courageous, that you may observe to do according to all the law which Moses My servant commanded you; do not turn from it to the right hand or to the left, that you may prosper wherever you go. This Book of the Law shall not depart from your mouth, but you shall meditate in it day and night, that you may observe to do according to all that is written in it. For then you will make your way prosperous, and then you will have good success. Have I not commanded you? Be strong and of good courage; do not be afraid, nor be dismayed, for the LORD your God is with you wherever you go. (Joshua 1:5–9)

God was not giving a gift; He was giving *Himself*.

God gave Joshua the greatest assurance He could give: "I will not leave you nor forsake you." God could have promised Joshua continuous victory. He could have guaranteed him protection or wisdom. He could have even provided Joshua with state of the art weapons for his soldiers. But when God pledged to Joshua His presence, He was offering him everything Joshua needed to be successful at every undertaking. God was not giving a gift; He was giving *Himself*.

Such an assurance left Joshua no cause for fear. Moreover, God said He would make His presence with Joshua obvious. Even Joshua's enemies would see it! (Josh. 2:9–11; 8:9–10, 24). "And the LORD said to Joshua, "This day I will begin to exalt you in the sight of all Israel, that they may know that, as I was with Moses, so I will be with you" (Josh. 3:7).

God immediately honored His promise. When the Israelites met their first major challenge under Joshua's leadership—crossing the Jordan River—God performed a spectacular miracle and brought them across on dry land (Josh. 3:15–17). Just as God had enabled Moses to master the barrier of the Red Sea, now God helped Joshua overcome the obstacle of the Jordan River.

When the people saw God's presence in Joshua's life just as they had witnessed it in Moses' life, they readily accepted Joshua's leadership. We read: "On that day the LORD exalted Joshua in the sight of all Israel; and they feared him, as they had feared Moses, all the days of his life" (Josh. 4:14). There is a profound life lesson here: God took care of Joshua's reputation. God exalted Joshua; Joshua didn't have to promote himself.

One of the most fruitless endeavors leaders undertake is to devote themselves to the promotion of their own reputations. Winston Churchill observed: "I know of no case where a man added to his dignity by standing on it."[9] When God chooses to humble a person, no amount of human exertion can erase God's sentence. Likewise, when God exalts someone, there is nothing critics and detractors can do to neutralize God's endorsement.

GOD EXALTS PEOPLE IN VARIOUS WAYS

What does it look like when God exalts a person? In Joshua's case, people grew to highly regard him. This was not a grudging respect Joshua insisted upon because of his position. If Joshua had reduced himself to demanding respect from the people, he wouldn't have deserved it in the first place. God developed in the hearts and minds of the Israelites a deep, abiding esteem for His servant Joshua.

God exalts people in various ways. He honored the prophet Samuel by ensuring every prophecy he uttered came to pass (1 Sam. 3:19–20). He upheld Elijah by sending down fire when the beleaguered prophet called upon Him in front of the king and a host of hostile religious leaders (1 Kings 18:38). God protected Elisha's reputation when he was cruelly 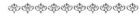 mocked by unruly youths (2 Kings 2:23–25). God blessed Job by giving him enormous wealth. God honored Moses in several ways, performing numerous spectacular miracles on his behalf.

> **If Joshua had reduced himself to demanding respect from the people, he wouldn't have deserved it in the first place.**

Perhaps the greatest attestation to God's close relationship with Moses was the way Moses' face shone every time he had been in God's presence (Ex. 34:29–30). Seeing Moses' face glow was evidence to everyone that he enjoyed God's favor! Joshua's face did not glow as Moses' did but he too communed intimately with God.

It is noteworthy that God exalted his servants in unique ways, according to their individual assignments. Moses had primarily been God's messenger to Pharaoh and to the Israelites. Joshua was a military commander. God affirmed Moses' role as His messenger by causing his face to shine after God instructed him. God certified Joshua as a military commander by giving him victory in every battle. (The only exception was when Achan's sin brought God's judgment, Josh. 7:10–26).

Just as the prophet Samuel's words always came to pass (1 Sam. 3:19), so Joshua emerged the victor in every conflict. People willingly deferred to Joshua's leadership because God's presence was evident by the outcome of every battle.

We have known men and women from all walks of life who reflected God's special presence and blessing. No doubt you have too. Business people, medical professionals, lawyers, and police officers have all testified to God's unique direction in their careers. Professional athletes have publicly attested to God's goodness. Parents have credited God for the blessing of children who wholeheartedly serve Christ as their Lord. Christian politicians have understood that God positioned them in a strategic place to make a godly impact on their nation.

God is looking for people today, just as He was in Joshua's day, who will trust Him, follow Him and give Him the glory for all He does in their lives. God's presence in a life is powerful and unmistakable!

JOSHUA POSSESSED THE SPIRIT OF WISDOM

What difference can God's Spirit make in a life? Joshua received the Spirit of wisdom and he was undefeatable (Num. 27:18). The Spirit took him beyond mere knowledge, giving him specific guidance to make the wisest decisions. God took the guesswork out of leadership for Joshua.

Joshua's willingness to trust God's wisdom, rather than his own knowledge, opened the floodgates of God's heavenly resources. Being able to recognize

God's voice allowed Joshua to hear all God had to tell him. This gave Joshua a decisive advantage, both on the battlefield and off. That's the difference God's Spirit makes.

> **God took the guesswork out of leadership for Joshua.**

The great seduction for many Christian leaders is to exalt their own intelligence and their ability for rational thought to a level God never intends. The insightful Benjamin Franklin said: "So convenient a thing it is to be a *reasonable creature*, since it enables one to find or make a reason for every thing one has a mind to do."[10] Often doing the reasonable thing is little more than an excuse to do what we think best without seeking the mind of the Lord on the subject. Woe to the organization that is guided merely by the best thinking of its leader!

Isaiah foretold that one day the Messiah would have God's Spirit upon Him:

> The Spirit of the LORD shall rest upon Him, The Spirit of wisdom and understanding, The Spirit of counsel and might, The Spirit of knowledge and of the fear of the LORD. His delight is in the fear of the LORD, And He shall not judge by the sight of His eyes, Nor decide by the hearing of His ears; But with righteousness He shall judge the poor, And decide with equity for the meek of the earth; He shall strike the earth with the rod of His mouth, And with the breath of His lips He shall slay the wicked. Righteousness shall be the belt of His loins, And faithfulness the belt of His waist. (Isaiah 11:2–5)

The Spirit of wisdom is a profound gift for those who desire it and seek it. Those upon whom the Spirit rests need not face situations with their own limited wisdom and understanding. They do not have to determine the reality of their situation based on what their eyes see or their ears hear. They are not restricted to their physical senses or their own best logic. They have the counsel and wisdom of God available to them. Joshua made good use of this wisdom and the results speak for themselves.

JOSHUA MEDITATED ON GOD'S WORD

Meditation hardly seems like the work of an industrious general. Yet God commanded Joshua to do just that if he hoped to succeed:

> Only be strong and very courageous, that you may observe to do according to all the law which Moses My servant commanded you; do not turn from it to the right hand or to the left, that you may prosper wherever you go. This Book of the Law shall not depart from your mouth, but you shall meditate in it day and night, that you may observe to do according to all that is written in it. For then you will make your way prosperous, and then you will have good success. (Joshua 1:7–8)

But how could a busy general command an army and administer a nation and still have time to meditate on anything? The hectic days would hardly afford opportunities for prolonged thought, let alone deep meditation. But God's command to meditate only sounds strange to the one who has never meditated.

MEDITATION

Meditation is focused concentration. It does not require a lonely mountaintop or a convoluted body position. It does not call for a trance or a mystical chant. Biblical meditation involves pondering God's Word until He makes its full implication clear. It is staying in God's presence until God has helped you understand what His Word is saying to you.

Woe to the organization that is guided merely by the best thinking of its leader!

Some biblical truths are self-evident; others require the Holy Spirit's illumination. A surface skimming of God's Word will not suffice for a leader who bears great responsibility. Too much is at stake. Only a careful, thoughtful period of meditation will ensure that leaders grasp all the ramifications of God's Word for those they lead.

Paradoxically, busy leaders facing significant time

pressures assume they have no time to meditate on God's Word. Time is precious. Yet the wisest thing a spiritual leader can do is to seek God's wisdom. Careful evaluation of God's Word is a must for the sake of everyone involved. It is the leader's responsibility to help their people understand God's promises and respond to His invitations.

> **Meditation is focused concentration . . . biblical meditation involves pondering God's Word until He makes its full implication clear.**

Busy leaders are people of action—others depend on them for prompt and timely decision-making. Yet history's greatest leaders have been able to screen out all distractions and to give their undivided attention to the issue at hand. Winston Churchill's biographer described his "fury of concentration. When his mind was occupied with a particular problem, however detailed, it focused upon it relentlessly. Nobody could turn him aside."[11]

Ellis Slater, one of Dwight Eisenhower's friends, noted: "I don't believe I've ever known a person with such concentration . . . he has an ability to completely lose himself."[12] Eisenhower's motto was: "Make no mistakes in a hurry."[13] The famous general took time to carefully consider what action he should take. As a military commander in a time of war, Eisenhower knew only too well that a hasty or careless decision could cost people their lives.

Likewise, spiritual leaders recognize that an unevaluated decision can bring disastrous and long-lasting consequences. The most potent tool at a spiritual leader's disposal is relentless, focused concentration on God's Word.

No crisis is pressing enough to prevent a leader from seeking God's perspective. A harried schedule should never hold a leader captive. Everyone is busy. But wise leaders understand the importance of meditation. They are proactive in scheduling time to focus, uninterrupted, on important issues.

The Bible is a storehouse packed full of wisdom. Unpacking its treasures takes time. God's Word holds answers leaders desperately need. The Scriptures can shed light on any situation. Why would a leader be foolhardy enough to ignore such a treasury of wisdom?

God told Joshua: "Be strong and of good courage; do not be afraid, nor be dismayed, for the LORD your God is with you wherever you go" (Josh. 1:9).

Was this important for Joshua to know? Absolutely. He was about to attempt the impossible. Thousands of people depended on him. He needed God to give him more than a sentimental, devotional thought. He needed a word from God that he could stake his life on.

Joshua ruminated over God's promise of His presence, meditating upon its practical implications. The coming days would bring numerous opportunities for fear and dismay. He had to be certain of the guarantees God had given him. Jesus made a similar promise to believers. He said, "and lo, I am with you always" (Matt. 28:20).

We need to grasp the enormity of this truth. How does this play out at our workplace? What does it mean when we are admitted to the hospital? Is it still true when everyone seems to have abandoned us? How does this work practically in day-to-day situations? How can I know God hasn't forsaken me when everything in my life is going wrong? The Bible holds promises with enormous implications if we would take time to consider their potential to revolutionize our lives. Joshua did and that is why he was so successful.

JOSHUA WAITED ON THE LORD

Leaders usually abhor waiting. They are typically doers. Most leaders would rather engage in *any* activity as long as they don't have to remain still! Waiting on God is different though. It *is* an activity, with a profound outcome. When you assume you must ultimately solve the problem or resolve the issue yourself, you feel compelled to take action. Knowing that God is responsible for the outcome of a situation or problem can turn waiting on Him into a relief. The response you make is determined by your view of God.

Waiting on God is actually a divine summons. It calls on the leader to acknowledge who is really in control. Waiting on God does not prescribe inactivity. Rather, it is an act of faith and obedience. Seeking God's direction takes more stamina than merely jumping rashly into action. If you think it doesn't take much effort to wait on the Lord, try it some time! In every situation there is both a right thing to do and a right time to do it. Waiting on the Lord helps leaders get them both right!

King Saul revealed his spiritual immaturity by  impatiently taking matters into his own hands rather than waiting on God. His brashness was his undoing (1 Sam. 13:1–14). God told him not to fight the Philistines until the prophet Samuel arrived to offer a sacrifice. A week went by with no 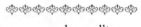 sign of Samuel. Saul's soldiers nervously watched the enemy ranks swelling.

Waiting on God is actually a divine summons.

This was a litmus test of Saul's faith. How seriously did he take a word from God? Did he understand that, even though he was the king, he could do *nothing* apart from God's strength? As the days passed, Saul's ranks diminished as more and more fearful soldiers deserted camp.

Finally, Saul couldn't stand it any more. He took action himself and offered the sacrifice to God in his own way, rather than the manner God had prescribed. His decision made sense to him, but it was a fatal error. In refusing to wait on God, Saul forfeited his right to be king.

Waiting on God is certainly a character-building exercise! Busy people are inundated with the voices of friends, colleagues, and clients. It takes an intentional effort to tune out every voice except God's. But personal and spiritual growth is the reward for doing so.

PROCRASTINATION AND WAITING ON THE LORD ARE DIFFERENT

A word of clarification is in order here. *Procrastination* and *waiting on the Lord* are two very different things. Elizabeth I was "a mistress of the subtle art of procrastination, she was marvelously adept at delaying and dissembling, and would usually shelve problems she could not immediately solve."[14]

Sometimes the biggest obstacle for a spiritual leader is not the problem itself, but the temptation to solve it alone. Spiritual leaders depend on a word from God. Without one they may be good leaders but they will not be spiritual leaders. Spiritual leaders take God's word and lead their followers to obey it. When a spiritual leader waits on God, a divine directive will come. And when it does, what the leader does next is critical.

Joshua was wise enough to understand that God knew far more than he did. Moreover, Joshua knew God intended to intervene on his behalf. It was

> **Sometimes the biggest obstacle for a spiritual leader is not the problem itself, but the temptation to solve it alone.**

therefore crucial to act in accordance with God's agenda. Doing things God's way would literally save thousands of soldiers' lives.

But how do you wait on the Lord if you don't know what He is saying? The most important factor in waiting on the Lord is hearing from Him in the first place. Joshua spent a significant amount of his time seeking God's will. He was an early riser. In those quiet morning hours God spoke to His servant (Josh. 3:1; 6:12; 7:16; 8:10).

God does not exist to serve us. He does not shadow us, requesting an audience at our convenience. Joshua regularly made himself available to God, and God communicated with him. Each day brought significant challenges to the Israelites; they needed a leader who had been in the Lord's presence and knew His will. They depended on Joshua to trust in God's timing to help them.

PERFECT TIMING

Obedience means saying yes immediately, but it does not always call for immediate action. God's timing is perfect. A good work performed too early or too late can be more damaging than no work at all. Abraham rushed the birth of an heir and it has cost his descendents ever since (Gen. 16:1–16).

The disciple Peter impetuously took a misguided stand for Jesus in the Garden of Gethsemane and all he received for his devotion was a slave's ear and a rebuke from his Master (John 18:10–11). Joshua had to wait forty years before going into the promised land, but when he finally entered to God's timing, his forces became invincible. The reward for waiting on God far exceeds the investment of patience required to do so.

JOSHUA PRAYED

It has been said that Mary, Queen of Scots, once lamented that she feared the prayers of the venerable John Knox more than all the armies of her enemies. Modern leaders are known for a variety of things, but prayer is generally not one of them. Like waiting on God, prayer is often mistaken for inactivity. You have probably heard the phrase: "If you can't do anything else (give money, go to the mission field, and so forth), you can always pray!"

Prayer should never be viewed as a substitute for something of consequence. It is the most practical and effective thing people can do. Yet busy leaders with hectic lives often consider prayer a luxury. Therefore it is often the first thing jettisoned once their calendars reach a saturation point. There are many administrators, but pitifully few intercessors.

> There are many administrators, but pitifully few intercessors.

Joshua was a man of habitual prayer. When Israel suffered a demoralizing defeat against the city of Ai, Joshua's first response was to humbly seek God's explanation (Josh. 7:6–9). Joshua carefully processed his failure through prayer. God responded by revealing the reason for their loss and providing the means for victory (Josh. 7:10–15).

In the midst of a fierce battle against the Amorites, Joshua prayed for God to intervene in nature. Again, God responded, holding the sun in place and enabling the Israelites to gain a decisive victory (Josh. 10:12–14). Joshua was not a prophet or a priest. His primary ministry was not one of intercession. He was a general leading a dangerous and complicated invasion; but not even Moses, the great prophets Isaiah and Jeremiah, or powerful preachers like Peter and Paul ever saw the sun and moon affected in answer to their prayers!

Joshua's prayers were not spoken in generalities. He asked God to meet specific, tangible needs. And when God answered miraculously, Joshua received the answer not with surprise, but as a matter of course. The children of Israel must have gained a deep reverence for their leader who communed with God so confidently. They saw in Joshua the kind of meaningful, pragmatic prayer life that characterizes a true spiritual leader.

DWIGHT MOODY: A MAN OF PRAYER

Dwight Moody was one of the greatest preachers of the nineteenth century. He had an incredible capacity for accomplishing numerous tasks in a short time. A popular riddle and answer circulated about him: "Why is D. L. so good?" "Because he drives so fast the Devil can't catch him!"[15]

Once he visited two hundred homes on New Year's Day. With such a hectic lifestyle his prayer life, though rich, was quite simple. Moody voiced short prayers throughout the day. When Moody faced a need, he prayed. His prayers seemed scandalously brief to some because he did not pray verbose, pedantic prayers. His prayers were simple and straightforward. And God always answered. On one occasion he admitted trying to pray all night as Martin Luther had purportedly done. D. L. confessed to awakening the next morning "a very stiff Moody."[16]

Joshua carefully processed his failure through prayer.

Those closest to him claimed they never heard him express long prayers but they heard him call on God often. Prayers need not be eloquently spoken or drawn out to epic length. The most profound prayers are expressed humbly and expectantly. Joshua prayed such prayers and miracles were a regular occurrence in his life.

JOSHUA HEARD GOD'S VOICE

It's quite obvious that God spoke to Joshua—often (Josh. 1:1; 3:7; 4:15; 5:15; 7:10; 8:1–2; 11:6; 13:1; 20:1). Joshua received a steady flow of specific instructions from God. This called on Joshua and his people for obedient responses. As they consistently obeyed God, they regularly experienced victory. Throughout the book of Joshua we find the following pattern: God spoke—Joshua obeyed—Joshua experienced success.

GOD SPEAKS

Many people, including some Bible scholars, claim that although God spoke to people like Joshua during biblical times, He does not speak to people today.[17] Some say the Bible contains all the instructions people need; God's commands, along with the biblical principles found in Scripture, negate the need for a direct word from God.

However, many times you will face a situation where there is no specific command to apply to your circumstances. No biblical principle specifically tells you whether you should lay off employees when the economy hits a downturn. Neither is there a particular commandment to guide you to know whether you should take a certain business trip or fill a vacant volunteer position.

Those who follow God's law and look to biblical principles for their guidance are certain to find direction. But they will still miss out on the *relationship* they could have enjoyed as God applied His word directly to their life. For example, say you are invited to take a new job in a different city. Your teenage son is going through a tortuous time of spiritual questioning and rebellion. Would a new school and church bring a fresh start, or additional stress? Moving might bring your family to a dynamic new church and youth group; then again, it might not.

You seek biblical principles to help guide your decision. You have a spouse and other children so your decision is complex. There are relevant biblical principles regarding both parenting and stewardship. You are confused. Which principle applies here? Does one principle take precedence over another? More than anything, you want a clear word from God. There is a lot at stake here! Your family cannot afford for you to make a mistake.

Joshua frequently faced this type of situation. Because he was a leader, his decisions would have dramatic ramifications on others. He knew his thinking was not on the same level as God's (Isa. 55:8–9). So Joshua regularly spoke with God and that's where he gained his perspective.

Scripture reveals that long before Joshua's time, God spoke to people. The book of Genesis tells of God speaking to people and many centuries after Joshua's time, the book of Revelation records  God still communing with people. He spoke in numerous ways, but clearly He communicated with people. And He *still* does. The testimony of the saints through the centuries up to and including today is that God still pursues a personal relationship with His children and He desires to give them His guidance.

> **Joshua regularly spoke with God and that's where he gained his perspective.**

73

Exactly *how* God spoke to Joshua is a biblical mystery. Did He use an audible voice or did He prompt Joshua's mind and heart? Scripture simply says, "the Lord spoke to Joshua" (Josh. 1:1). Obviously *how* God spoke was not considered important. *That* God spoke was crucial. God found a way to communicate His will to Joshua, Joshua understood what God said, and Joshua always responded in obedience.

Several times God gave Joshua military strategies he would not have known otherwise. God also revealed the identity of the culprit in Jericho who violated God's restrictions (Josh. 7:10–26). Hearing from God gave Joshua a decided advantage over his idol-worshiping opponents.

Hearing from God also removed any doubts Joshua might have had when going into battle. Once God appointed Joshua as a leader, Joshua had no need to fill out a spiritual gifts questionnaire to determine if he was equipped to lead. It didn't matter! God had just commissioned him as a leader and would guide him in each step he took.

OBEDIENCE AND SUCCESS

Today there is an epidemic of evangelical idolatry. Idolatry is when people maintain substitutes for God. Rather than seeking him, they pursue a principle. They don't respond immediately to God's voice. First, they take an inventory to see if they have the skills necessary to be obedient! People are trusting in doctrine rather than in God. People are placing their faith in their own leadership skills or training or in personality tests, rather than in God's guidance. That's idolatry.

Many Christians struggle to obey God, not because they are defiant, but because they are unsure how to hear from Him. If they clearly heard His voice, they would do what He said. But when you are uncertain how to recognize God's voice, you can become hesitant, afraid of making a mistake. Joshua was so familiar with God's voice that one word from God was enough to move him confidently forward. Hearing God's voice was the crux of Joshua's success as a spiritual leader.

JOSHUA STUDIED GOD'S WAYS

Joshua's appointment as Israel's new leader came with a profound promise. God assured him: "As I was with Moses, so I will be with you" (Josh. 1:5). Wrapped up in this magnificent promise was a history of miracles and victories along with more than one instance of discipline. Joshua had witnessed all this in Moses' period of leadership. In light of this word from God, it certainly behooved Joshua to review how God had specifically related to Moses!

When God first spoke to Moses, He identified Himself in terms of how He had walked with Moses' predecessors. He said, "I am the God of your father—the God of Abraham, the God of Isaac, and the God of Jacob" (Ex. 3:6). God was declaring that He was the same God the earlier patriarchs had followed. He would walk with Moses as he had related to the patriarchs. God never changes (Mal. 3:6).

The specific method God used to speak to Moses might vary greatly from the ways He spoke to the patriarchs. Abraham, Isaac, and Jacob never encountered a burning bush! But if Moses carefully studied the way God dealt with his forefathers he would see that God would guide and sustain him too.

Now it was Joshua's turn. There was God's assurance He would make His presence obvious to Joshua. Joshua had witnessed the varied and unique ways He had manifested His presence to Moses. Now he would see God work mightily in his own life.

It is vitally important for Christians to study the Scriptures and to read biographies of Christians and spiritual leaders.[18] In so doing, we can learn much about the way God consistently deals with His people. God did not overlook the sin in Moses' or David's life, though they were major religious leaders of their day.

We can safely conclude that God will not overlook our sin either, regardless of what we may be doing in His service. Likewise, if God came to the aid of His servants Joshua, Gideon, and Elijah as they

> **Spiritual leaders are wise to carefully study the ways God has worked through people's lives in Scripture and in history.**

bravely took a stand for Him, we can assume He will also assist us in our challenges as we obediently serve Him.

Many of history's great leaders were avid history students. Queen Elizabeth I purposefully spent three hours a day reading history books.[19] Rather than being captive to her present circumstances, she wanted to view her present situation from the vantage point of all that had gone before.

Winston Churchill said, "If we quarrel with the past we may lose the future."[20] Dwight Eisenhower loved to read history.[21] Likewise, spiritual leaders are wise to carefully study the ways God has worked through people's lives in Scripture and in history so they know how God might use their lives for His kingdom as well.

We have plenty of reason to study the Scriptures. Through the millennia God has worked powerfully through the lives of ordinary people. God's activity in the lives of His people is evident not only in biblical history, but throughout two thousand years of Christian history as well. We should confidently assume that just as God was with Moses and David and Peter and Paul, so He will be with us.

CONCLUSION

Joshua had many skills and talents that helped him to function effectively as a leader. Yet those skills alone cannot explain his phenomenal success. Only God can. God's presence was unmistakably obvious, not only to God's people but even to unbelievers. And that presence made all the difference.

As Joshua yielded himself to God's guidance, God was pleased to use his life for His divine purposes. God often spoke to Joshua and made sure he knew His will. Joshua meditated upon the words God spoke. Joshua knew that his life, and the lives of his countrymen, depended upon his understanding and obeying God's word.

Joshua prayed regularly. He waited upon God. He observed how God walked with those who had gone before him. He sought to have a close walk with God himself. Joshua was not satisfied with anything less than God's manifest presence in his life. And God was active in Joshua's life. The

Scriptures bear testimony to the astounding success God's presence made in the life of one servant who listened to Him and obeyed what he heard.

GOD'S PRESENCE: THE SECRET TO SUCCESS

- Joshua exercised good leadership.
- Joshua received God's affirmation.
- Joshua possessed the Spirit of wisdom.
- Joshua meditated on God's Word.
- Joshua waited on the Lord.
- Joshua prayed.
- Joshua heard God's voice.
- Joshua studied God's ways.

QUESTIONS FOR CONSIDERATION

1. Are you currently experiencing spiritual barrenness as Duncan Campbell did? If so, what are you doing to remedy your spiritual condition?

2. Is God affirming you in your present leadership role? If so, what is the evidence God is pleased with your current leadership performance?

3. How have you relied on the "Spirit of wisdom" in your leadership responsibilities?

4. How often do you meditate on God's Word? How could you incorporate more time for meditation in your life?

5. Are you presently waiting on the Lord? How have you been handling the waiting period?

6. Do you recognize God's voice? What have you heard Him say lately?

FIVE

OBEDIENCE THAT
GOES THE DISTANCE

THE WHOLE CASTLE WAS ASTIR. The monarch was paying a long-awaited royal visit. Elaborate preparations had consumed the preceding months. A newly constructed tower stood ready, furnished with royal apartments to house the sovereign upon her visit. The Earl of Leicester, lord of the castle, rode out to meet his beloved queen. Much pomp and pageantry ensued. Seven miles from the castle he had erected a luxurious pavilion, and there he furnished his sovereign and her entourage with a sumptuous dinner.

As they finally approached the castle, the queen could see the massive structure illuminated by thousands of torches and candles. The pillars of the drawbridge were elaborately adorned with fruit and vines. Hanging on the vines were musical instruments and armor, all latent with meaning. A "floating island" appeared in the moat and lavishly decorated characters humbly offered the queen the keys to the castle.

As the monarch entered her royal suite, guns were fired and fireworks set off. It is said that when the queen mentioned her disappointment to her host that she could not view the formal garden from her window, the mortified earl hastily conscripted an army of laborers and constructed an identical garden outside her window overnight![1]

Who was this monarch, the recipient of such elaborate homage? Queen Elizabeth I. She would spend ten days at the famous castle at Kenilworth in July 1575. Each day boasted a unique feast or performance offered in her honor. A single banquet showcased over one thousand pieces of glass and silver. Two hundred gentlemen served three hundred exquisite dishes.

It was an age when reverence for the monarch was practiced to spectacular extremes. Some nobles actually redesigned their homes so they would form the shape of an "E" in honor of their revered queen.[2] Nobles wishing to speak to the queen at her court would humbly approach her on their knees. Should one of her courtiers wish to speak with her, they would patiently wait for an opportunity when the queen might pass by them and then respectfully say, "God save your majesty, I crave your ear at what hour may suit for your servant to meet your blessed countenance."[3] Reverence for the queen was paramount.

Reverence is the ultimate expression of respect and a cause for abject humility. While the Earl of Leicester may have been partly motivated by a desire to impress the queen, he was also driven by the realization he was receiving the most powerful person in the land.

Joshua was a respected general, the nation's top leader, yet he understood clearly his role as a servant of God. He never confused who the leader was in his relationship with his Lord. Joshua demonstrated a radical subservience to the commands of his King. Joshua yielded to God, obeyed God, accepted hard assignments, and Joshua's obedience was unflinching.

JOSHUA YIELDED TO GOD

An unusual event in Joshua's life occurred on the eve of his famous attack on Jericho:

> And it came to pass, when Joshua was by Jericho, that he lifted his eyes and looked, and behold, a Man stood opposite him with His sword drawn in His hand. And Joshua went to Him and said to Him, "Are You for us or for our adversaries?" So He said, "No, but as Commander of the army of the LORD I have now come." And Joshua fell on his face to the earth and worshiped, and said to Him, "What does my Lord say to His servant?" Then the Commander of the LORD's army said to Joshua, "Take your sandal off your foot, for the place where you stand is holy." And Joshua did so. (Joshua 5:13–15)

Jericho symbolized the very thing that had terrified ten Hebrew spies forty years earlier. It was a walled city protected by menacing soldiers. It looked invincible. Jericho was the ultimate test for the Israelites. They had finally entered the promised land but they had yet to fight the enemy. The following day would bring the first major test to this generation of Israelite warriors.

The evening before the battle, Joshua carefully surveyed the fortified city. His gaze suddenly fell upon an impressive looking soldier with sword in hand. A drawn sword indicated battle-readiness. Joshua boldly confronted the stranger to determine if he was friend or foe.

Joshua discovered the stranger was neither for Jericho nor for Israel—he was God's servant. Joshua's heavenly visitor was commander of the Lord's army. A military man, Joshua immediately recognized one who carried greater authority than he. Joshua stood before one who far outranked him and whose army was infinitely more powerful than his.

Their interchange is reminiscent of two similar biblical encounters. Jacob met a heavenly messenger one night as he waited at the ford of the river Jabbock to meet his estranged brother Esau. Unlike Joshua, Jacob wrestled with his divine visitor all evening (Gen. 32:22–32). For whatever reason, when confronted with God's messenger, Jacob's first impulse was to fight.

Likewise, when Moses encountered God in a burning bush, his natural instinct was to resist. Moses argued against God's will until he provoked the Lord's anger (Ex. 4:14). Jacob was a deceiver—a conniver who sought the advantage over others. Moses lacked confidence. He was aware of his many inadequacies and he was convinced God was making a mistake by calling him into His service.

Joshua's military experience taught him to recognize authority. He knew subordinates did not argue with their superiors. The moment he recognized whose presence he was in, there was no wrestling or arguing. There was only obedience.

RESISTING GOD'S WILL IS COSTLY

Resisting God is a costly venture. For the remainder of his life, Jacob's limping gait was a visible reminder of his stubbornness (Gen. 32:31). Moses had to speak for God through Aaron throughout the rest of his ministry (Ex. 4:14–16).

On the other hand, God chose to mightily bless Joshua's leadership throughout his life.

Life affords numerous opportunities for believers to prove their allegiance to God. The same God who encountered Jacob, Moses, Joshua, and dozens of other Bible characters, confronts each Christian with His will.

Resistance always comes at a price. Scores of troubled people have shared with us that God called them into ministry, but they resisted and put off their ministerial training for numerous "practical" reasons. They spent their lives on the sidelines when they knew they should be serving God in full-time ministry.

God prompted others to restore broken relationships but their pride prevented reconciliation until it was too late. Fortunately, God is gracious and He will restore us if we will obey what we know He is asking us to do today. But many lost opportunities are irretrievable.

LEARNING A HARD LESSON

Mel Blackaby is Henry and Marilynn Blackaby's third son. As a teenager he knew his two older brothers were both called into full-time Christian ministry. Mel came to realize God was calling him as well—but he resisted. He was having too much fun to get serious about the Lord. Rather than focusing on college and preparing for seminary, he rationalized that he needed time to earn money. He had aspirations of buying a nice car and having fun with his friends for a time before settling down to the serious business of serving the Lord.

He pulled out of school for a semester and took a well-paid job at a logging camp. It was only to be a temporary diversion. But, while logging, Mel was terribly injured in a freak accident. He shattered one leg and came perilously close to death. Bedridden for months and suffering incredible pain, he knew his moneymaking plans had come to naught. He ended up losing two semesters of school and had only a damaged leg to show for it.

Once he recovered, Mel returned to his studies, eventually earning his Ph.D. Today he is the pastor of a leading church in Canada and has coauthored two books with his father.[4] His books are encouraging thousands of people around the world. He is grateful to God for redirecting his life, but he learned a hard lesson about resisting God's will.

The New Testament tells of a man in Jesus' day who, much like Joshua, displayed remarkable faith (Matt. 8:5–13). A Gentile centurion approached Jesus on behalf of his ailing servant. Jesus offered to accompany the noble soldier to heal his servant, but the man humbly demurred:

> Lord, I am not worthy that You should come under my roof. But only speak a word, and my servant will be healed. For I also am a man under authority, having soldiers under me. And I say to this one, "Go," and he goes; and to another, "Come," and he comes; and to my servant, "Do this," and he does it. (Matthew 8:8–9)

This man recognized authority! For such men there is no begrudging or questioning a superior's commands. There is only submission. Jesus was amazed at the veteran soldier's faith and richly rewarded his servitude (Matt. 8:10, 13).

People sometimes speak of "wrestling" with God: "I know God wants me to lead a Bible study in my home but I have been wrestling with Him about it because I don't feel adequate for the task." Or, "I sense God wants me to accept a job transfer but I have been wrestling with Him because it means moving away from my friends and relatives."

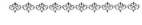

> **God is not an equal to be resisted. He is God and we must yield to Him.**

Wrestling is not a legitimate step in the process of seeking God's will. It is blatant disobedience. Those who speak of wrestling with God do not know Him. God is not an equal to be resisted. He is God and we must yield to Him.

GOD'S NATURE

To respond appropriately to God's will we must understand His nature. *God is love* (1 John 4:8). He cannot and will not act out of any motive but perfect love. Everything God will ever say to you is an expression of His love. Even when He disciplines you and convicts you of your sin, it is because He loves you (Heb. 12:6–7). Why would anyone resist an expression of perfect love? It is ludicrous, to say nothing of costly, to argue with Him.

God is omniscient. He is all knowing. He sees the future. He understands our past and our present in minute detail. His wisdom is infinite. To what purpose would anyone argue with a God such as this?

Finally, God is omnipotent. He is all-powerful. Consider the words of the apostle John as he described his vision of the risen Christ upon His throne:

> Immediately I was in the Spirit; and behold, a throne set in heaven, and One sat on the throne. And He who sat there was like a jasper and a sardius stone in appearance; and there was a rainbow around the throne, in appearance like an emerald. Around the throne were twenty-four thrones, and on the thrones I saw twenty-four elders sitting, clothed in white robes; and they had crowns of gold on their heads. And from the throne proceeded lightnings, thunderings, and voices. Seven lamps of fire were burning before the throne, which are the seven Spirits of God. Before the throne there was a sea of glass, like crystal. And in the midst of the throne, and around the throne, were four living creatures full of eyes in front and in back. The first living creature was like a lion, the second living creature like a calf, the third living creature had a face like a man, and the fourth living creature was like a flying eagle. The four living creatures, each having six wings, were full of eyes around and within. And they do not rest day or night, saying:
>
> "Holy, holy, holy, Lord God Almighty, Who was and is and is to come!"
>
> Whenever the living creatures give glory and honor and thanks to Him who sits on the throne, who lives forever and ever, the twenty-four elders fall down before Him who sits on the throne and worship Him who lives forever and ever, and cast their crowns before the throne, saying:
>
> "You are worthy, O Lord, To receive glory and honor and power; For You created all things, And by Your will they exist and were created." (Revelation 4:2–11)

Is there any mention of resistance or struggle? Of course not. That would be absurd! The Lord of heaven and earth is exalted upon His throne. No one complains that they are not gifted to sing "Holy, Holy, Holy!" No one begrudges the length of the worship service. No one insists they cannot afford to cast their crowns at His feet. In heaven, the saints will humbly worship and obey their Lord not because they have to, but because when they see God as He truly is, no other response will cross their minds!

We mortals have yet to gaze upon our risen Lord. The evidence of His existence and greatness is everywhere around us, but it still requires faith to believe Him and to obey Him. Some feel they can argue with God because they have yet to learn what He is truly like. However, those who really come to know Christ will deny themselves, take up their crosses, and follow Him (Matt. 10:37–39; 16:24–25; Luke 14:26–27). No other response befits a follower of Christ (Isa. 6:1–5).

JOSHUA OBEYED GOD

Joshua was not a halfhearted believer. His thoroughness is evident in an event that occurred after the Israelites crossed the Jordan River into Canaan. God told Joshua to circumcise all the Israelite males (Josh. 5:2). The Hebrew children born during the forty years of wandering in the wilderness had not been circumcised as their fathers had.

Before God would use them to establish a nation in Canaan, He wanted all the men to physically bear the sign of His covenant with them. From a pragmatic perspective, this does not appear to be the best timing for such an exercise in obedience. Circumcising all the adult males after having just entered enemy territory would have left the army vulnerable to attack.

Joshua might have been excused for waiting for a safer and more convenient time to take care of this issue. But his primary concern was not safety or convenience; it was obedience. Joshua wisely concluded the best place for his army was in the center of God's will.

His primary concern was not safety or convenience; it was obedience.

Since God first established His covenant with Abraham (Gen. 17:10–14), circumcision signified that a Hebrew male belonged to God's people. Other nations also practiced circumcision, but usually on adults and for other reasons. Abraham's descendents were all to be circumcised as infants and to grow up with the physical reminder that they belonged to God.

Moses was meticulous in most areas of his walk with God, but he seems to have lapsed in the area of circumcision. After meeting with God at the burning bush, Moses traveled toward Egypt. On the way, God almost took his life because he had failed to circumcise his son:

> And it came to pass on the way, at the encampment, that the LORD met him and sought to kill him. Then Zipporah took a sharp stone and cut off the foreskin of her son and cast it at Moses' feet, and said, "Surely you are a husband of blood to me!" So He let him go. Then she said, "You are a husband of blood!"—because of the circumcision. (Exodus 4:24–26)

Moses' wife Zipporah was a Midianite. Midianites circumcised adult males just before their wedding. Perhaps Moses was putting off his son's circumcision until his wedding day to satisfy his wife. Whatever the reason, God expected the leader of His people to adhere to His commands. Failing to do so almost cost Moses his life.

It's not clear whether God explicitly commanded circumcision of Hebrew children during the forty years they lived in the desert, but none of the Israelites were circumcised during Moses' term of leadership. In light of Moses' failure to have his son or any of the other males circumcised, Joshua's immediate obedience to God's instruction is even more impressive. He understood that circumcision represented the peoples' commitment to God's covenant.

Before they invaded the promised land, every man was to signify his total commitment to God. In calling for every male's circumcision, Joshua surely encountered some resistance. He also risked his popularity as a leader. But when it came to following God's commands, Joshua was single-minded.

JOSHUA ACCEPTED HARD ASSIGNMENTS

Two important truths Joshua lived by are two of the most difficult realities for modern Christians to understand and accept: 1) God will eventually judge everyone who sins against Him; 2) God commands His people to remain separate from spiritual rebels lest they be drawn into the same destructive lifestyle that inevitably brings about God's judgment. Only by clearly understanding the importance of both these truths can we appreciate what God told Joshua to do to the inhabitants of Canaan.

Joshua's job, as happens in all leadership positions, put him into some tough situations. The times in which he lived were barbaric and life was often extremely difficult. As the Israelites approached Jericho, God commanded them to refrain from taking any plunder after their victory. Everything in Jericho—their first conquest in Canaan—was to be dedicated to God as a holy offering to God (Josh. 6:18–19). Every living thing within Jericho was to be destroyed, except for Rahab and her relatives (Josh. 6:22–23).

God's command appears unduly harsh to us and seemingly far removed from the love Jesus showed the notorious sinner Zacchaeus and the gentle forgiveness the Savior offered the adulterous woman (Luke 19:1–10; John 8:1–11). Why would the same loving God instruct His people to withhold mercy from their Canaanite foes?

It seems to fly in the face of Jesus' command to love our enemies (Matt. 5:38–45). Yet there is a vast difference between the manner in which Jesus commanded His disciples to respond to personal injuries and the way God dealt with nations that repeatedly defied His holy standards.

Canaan was infested with idolatry and the grossest forms of immorality. The people embraced idol worship to hideous extremes. Farmers desiring rain for their crops and a lucrative harvest would sacrifice their own children on an altar in an effort to win their idol's favor. Their depraved worship included prostitution and immoral acts as a part of the religious services.

The pagan religion encouraged every carnal and debased practice God had condemned. Canaanite worship was the vulgar antithesis of what holy God prescribed for His people. Unless the people of Canaan repented, God would ultimately judge them.

God made a prophetic statement to Abraham centuries earlier that would eventually come to pass in Joshua's day. God was fully aware of the moral and spiritual depravity of the Amorites who inhabited the promised land. God told Abraham his descendents would suffer a difficult sojourn in a distant country for four hundred years, "for the iniquity of the Amorites is not yet complete" (Gen. 15:16).

God was being merciful to the inhabitants of Canaan. Their blatant sensuality was an abomination to His holiness. Yet God declared that their sins had not yet reached full maturity, the point at which God's righteousness would demand punishment. In fact, God granted them four hundred additional years to turn from the wickedness of their ways.

Only an infinitely gracious and loving God who does not desire that anyone perish would be so lenient (2 Peter 3:9). In our day, it is sobering to realize Christ has delayed His final return and judgment for two thousand years so that every person has the opportunity to respond to His love and to be saved from the consequences of his or her sin.

By the time Joshua arrived in Canaan with the Israelites, the Canaanites' opportunity to repent was finally exhausted. Joshua and his soldiers were to be the instruments of God's judgment on a people who mocked and rejected Him, even after centuries of receiving His mercy.

God did not always command the Israelites to exterminate everyone they fought. This was not the routine way Israelite armies treated their enemies once they inhabited Canaan. Often people would be given the opportunity to surrender and, if they did not, women and children would still generally be spared.

Yet God intended for Jericho, the first city, to be utterly destroyed. Not only was God determined to judge the sinful inhabitants and to strike paralyzing fear in the hearts of their allies, He was also deeply concerned that Israel not be morally or spiritually contaminated by the influence of the idol-worshiping Canaanites.

God repeatedly urged His people not to intermarry with those who practiced pagan religions. Marrying outside their faith would have a spiritually deadening effect upon his people. God commanded them:

> Do not defile yourselves with any of these things; for by all these the nations are defiled, which I am casting out before you. For the land is defiled; therefore I visit the punishment of its iniquity upon it, and the land vomits out its

inhabitants. You shall therefore keep My statutes and My judgments, and shall not commit any of these abominations, either any of your own nation or any stranger who dwells among you (for all these abominations the men of the land have done, who were before you, and thus the land is defiled), lest the land vomit you out also when you defile it, as it vomited out the nations that were before you. For whoever commits any of these abominations, the persons who commit them shall be cut off from among their people. Therefore you shall keep My ordinance, so that you do not commit any of these abominable customs which were committed before you, and that you do not defile yourselves by them: I am the LORD your God. (Leviticus 18:24–30)

God's message both to His people and to the idolatrous Canaanites was clear and powerful. He was declaring total, implacable war on the sinful and idolatrous lifestyle of those who rejected Him. God left no room for discussion or compromise. If allowed to remain in Canaan, the idol-worshipers would be fierce enemies of the Israelites. They would have little interest in sharing Israel's religion. Instead they would provide enticing temptations for compromise and immorality.

Joshua eliminated the leading religious leaders of the idolatrous nations in Canaan. God was divesting the promised land of the idolatry that would tempt the Israelites toward their own destruction. It may seem incomprehensible that God used Joshua as an instrument to bring death to so many. But God's ways are not our ways (Isa. 55:8–9).

Throughout history God has used people as His instruments of judgment. When we question God's discipline we are elevating our own perspective above God's. When we trust God and rely on His sovereignty we will not second-guess His wisdom. However harsh God's actions may seem, He saw the need to judge flagrant rebellion and to protect His people from the many temptations awaiting them.

> **When we question God's discipline we are elevating our own perspective above God's.**

We must be careful not to think we are more compassionate and gracious to sinners than God is! We must also be cautious in placing our concern on

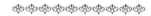

the side of the sinner rather than in the sovereignty of God. God is infinitely loving but He is also absolutely just. There comes a time when God will no longer delay bringing judgment on those who deserve it (Jer. 15:1).

It is a natural instinct to become uneasy when God disciplines someone. At times a church must respond firmly to a wayward member who blatantly sins and refuses to repent. The inevitable reaction of some members is, "Yes they sinned, but who hasn't? Who are we to judge? But for the grace of God we would do the same thing!"

Listen carefully: *compassion for a sinner is absolutely crucial, but misguided compassion can lead us to flagrantly oppose the work God is doing in our midst.* Excusing another's continuous rebellion actually harms them more than it helps them. Our concern ought to always be with God and His redemptive activity. We do not help fellow Christians by interfering when God is disciplining them.

Unequally Yoked

The New Testament also warns of the dangers of allowing sinners to corrupt God's people: "Do not be unequally yoked together with unbelievers. For what fellowship has righteousness with lawlessness? And what communion has light with darkness? And what accord has Christ with Belial? Or what part has a believer with an unbeliever?" (2 Cor. 6:14). Long after Joshua's time, God still commands his people not to link our lives with unbelievers lest they draw us away from our allegiance to God.

We have known parents who never taught their children the magnitude of this charge. When their child began dating an unbeliever, the parents did not urge them to break off their relationship and heed God's counsel. The well-meaning parents did not want to appear harsh or judgmental. After their child's marriage, the wisdom of God's warning became increasingly apparent.

> **While God's commands can sometimes seem demanding, they are always motivated by love and are always for our good.**

Significant differences of opinion arose between the young couple regarding how to raise the children,

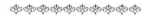

89

whether to attend church, how to use their money and what moral standards to establish for their home. The Christian spouse suffered the lonely experience of single-handedly carting the kids off to church week after week under the apathetic gaze of the unbelieving spouse. Eventually the fundamental differences in values and priorities led to a heartbreaking divorce.

The parents who thought God's injunction was too severe to impress on their child were forced to watch helplessly as their precious child and grandchildren suffered the agony of marriage breakdown. While God's commands can sometimes seem demanding, they are always motivated by love and they are always for our good.

Joshua was never squeamish about following God's most difficult commands. The Duke of Wellington once observed: "Nothing except a battle lost can be half so melancholy as a battle won."[5] When God instructed Joshua to bring total judgment on a city, he obeyed unquestioningly. Joshua was not a malicious, vindictive man who enjoyed destroying cities. But he understood that when God placed people under judgment, their punishment was to be thorough:

> But of the cities of these peoples which the LORD your God gives you as an inheritance, you shall let nothing that breathes remain alive, but you shall utterly destroy them: the Hittite and the Amorite and the Canaanite and the Perizzite and the Hivite and the Jebusite, just as the LORD your God has commanded you, lest they teach you to do according to all their abominations which they have done for their gods, and you sin against the LORD your God. (Deuteronomy 20:16–18)

After Jericho's destruction, God instructed Joshua to raze the nearby city of Ai. Joshua's forces were initially defeated because of sin in his ranks but Joshua attacked the small city a second time. Joshua informed his warriors that as long as he held up his javelin, they were to fight the enemy to the death.

Joshua held up his javelin until there were no enemy survivors (Josh. 8:25–26). Over and over again the book of Joshua tells us Joshua was called upon to leave no survivors (Josh. 6:24; 8:26; 10:20, 28; 11:14). To carry out such an onerous assignment, Joshua had to cling tightly to his unwavering faith in God's righteous wisdom.

JOSHUA'S OBEDIENCE WAS UNFLINCHING

When the Israelites approached Jericho, God declared the city under the ban—every living creature was to be destroyed and no loot was to be kept. Everything was to be a holy sacrifice to God. A man named Achan spied a beautiful garment and some silver and gold and he couldn't resist hiding them in his tent (Josh. 7:21). No one else knew of Achan's store of contraband.

It appeared the Israelites had been overwhelmingly successful. God miraculously brought the walls of Jericho crumbling down as He had promised. The Israelites quickly overcame the stunned resistors and the city fell into their hands. Yet, in the midst of the victory celebrations, Achan was surreptitiously stashing his loot. Some of the most costly sins are committed in the shadow of God's greatest works. Perhaps it was people such as Achan to whom the apostle John referred when he said, "They went out from us, but they were not of us" (1 John 2:19).

> **Some of the most costly sins are committed in the shadow of God's greatest works.**

We have all known of such situations—perhaps it was a congregation flourishing under God's blessing. Attendance was multiplying. People were coming to know Christ. Broken families were being restored. Mission projects were underway. Then came a stunning revelation—the pastor was involved in sexual immorality. Shock reverberated among the congregation and the community.

It seemed incomprehensible that someone in the center of God's redemptive activity could be tempted to sin so grievously. But it is possible, and tragically, it happens often. Leaders should never underestimate their own vulnerability to sin, even when they are at a point of great personal success. We always fall furthest from our highest point.

❀❀❀❀❀❀❀❀❀❀ Ananias and Sapphira were privileged to be
members of the first church in Jerusalem. They had

**Leaders should
never
underestimate their
own vulnerability
to sin.**

Peter, James, and John as their pastors and godly men
such as Stephen as their deacons. Three thousand
people were added to their church in just one day!
(Acts 2:41). Needless to say, God was working mightily! Miracles were a frequent occurrence.

❀❀❀❀❀❀❀❀❀❀ But in the midst of all of God's activity, this
couple was consumed with pride. They allowed their greed to overtake them
and it led them to publicly dishonor the Holy Spirit. The result was death
for them both (Acts 5:1–11). Committing blasphemy in the midst of God's
greatest work is the insidious work of sin in a person's heart.

Ananias's and Sapphira's consequences were instantaneous. Not so with
Achan. His sin remained hidden in his tent until the Israelites confronted
their next opponent, the city of Ai. This minor city should have presented
minimal challenge. Only a small contingent of Israelite soldiers was considered necessary to secure a victory. Yet to their profound dismay, the Israelites
were soundly defeated. This was Joshua's only recorded defeat and he didn't
take it well!

> Then Joshua tore his clothes, and fell to the earth on his face before the
> ark of the LORD until evening, he and the elders of Israel; and they put dust
> on their heads. And Joshua said, "Alas, Lord GOD, why have You brought
> this people over the Jordan at all—to deliver us into the hand of the
> Amorites, to destroy us? Oh, that we had been content, and dwelt on the
> other side of the Jordan! O Lord, what shall I say when Israel turns its back
> before its enemies? For the Canaanites and all the inhabitants of the land
> will hear it, and surround us, and cut off our name from the earth. Then
> what will You do for Your great name?" (Joshua 7:6–9)

Considering the Israelites only lost a few dozen men in the skirmish, Joshua's
response appears almost melodramatic. But Joshua's confidence in God had
been absolute. He fully believed that when God marched with him into bat-

tle, he was invincible. God had promised: "Every place that the sole of your foot will tread upon I have given you . . . no man shall be able to stand before you all the days of your life" (Josh. 1:3, 5).

The possibility of defeat never crossed Joshua's mind as long as he followed God's will. This setback deeply troubled him. He had obeyed God's instructions and was still defeated. What assurance was there for his future? Furthermore, when word spread across Canaan that it was indeed possible to defeat God's people, all their enemies would quickly attack them with a vengeance.

> **The possibility of defeat never crossed Joshua's mind as long as he followed God's will.**

The second half of God's promise was that if the Israelites were not faithful, he would ensure their continual loss in battle (Deut. 28:7, 25). Though Joshua was unaware of Achan's treachery, he now knew the bitter taste of defeat. Joshua must have been bewildered and horrified at the thought of having God as his enemy. Joshua's entire view of God was momentarily shaken. Then Joshua heard from God and, as always, that put everything into perspective.

God urged his despondent general: "Get up! Why do you lie thus on your face? Israel has sinned" (Josh. 7:10). Significantly, God did not say, "Achan has sinned." All of God's people were to face the consequences of one man's sin. God could have identified the culprit and Joshua could have discreetly punished him. Yet God caused the entire nation to go through the extremely public process of discovering the traitorous sinner.

Tribe by tribe, clan by clan, family by family, the people of Israel watched as God disclosed the guilty person and pronounced judgment on him: "Then it shall be that he who is taken with the accursed thing shall be burned with fire, he and all that he has, because he has transgressed the covenant of the LORD, and because he has done a disgraceful thing in Israel" (Josh. 7:15).

Everyone knew what was at stake for the one condemned. As the entire nation watched, they witnessed the gravity of sin. No one could miss the way God thoroughly and stringently treated the disobedience of

His people. God used this crisis as a profound deterrent for every Israelite household.

When God finally identified Achan as the culprit, Joshua was left with the incredibly difficult task of putting him and his family to death. Achan was from the tribe of Judah, of the Zarhites. He would have had many relatives and friends among the Israelites.

Surely the people were shaken by such a severe punishment. After all, the contraband had been discovered and the sin confessed. Yet God treated this disregard for His word with utmost severity. He made a dramatic example of Achan and left no room for doubt that His word was always to be treated with reverence and followed scrupulously.

Jericho had been the first enemy stronghold the Israelites had attacked in Canaan and already one of God's people had flagrantly sinned. If the Israelites were going to successfully conquer the promised land, they would have to be convinced that only total obedience was acceptable to God. Absolute compliance to God's word was the key to their success. And so God punished Achan in such a dramatic way that every Israelite got the message.

Obeying God's decree put Joshua in a heart-wrenching situation. Killing enemy soldiers in hand-to-hand combat was one thing. Slaying one of your own people was quite another. Everyone looked to Joshua to see what he would do. Moses had dealt with his share of detractors and critics. Joshua could be sure that if he acted, many people might consider him heartless and cruel. Yet not to follow through would gain him God's displeasure.

Joshua obviously feared God far more than he feared men. We see no hesitation. No questioning God (Josh. 7:24–26). In fact, on that morning Joshua rose early to begin the difficult job (Josh. 7:16). It was a harsh, gruesome task, but Joshua and the people did it promptly and completely.

> **It is a frightening thing for God to use the example of your life as a deterrent for others.**

After Achan's death, there is no record of a similar breach of obedience among God's people throughout the remainder of Joshua's leadership. It is a frightening thing for God to use the example of your life as a deterrent for others.

We are not at liberty to pick and choose which of God's commands we will obey. Some words from God are welcome and agreeable. Others call for great effort and sacrifice. Joshua never seems to have distinguished between the two. Whether the command was easy to carry out or whether it was arduous, Joshua was equally zealous.

JOSHUA SOMETIMES BLEW IT

It has been said that Queen Victoria enjoyed Benjamin Disraeli as prime minister much more than she liked William Gladstone because Gladstone often candidly disagreed with her while Disraeli never did. Although Disraeli did not argue with the commands of his temperamental monarch, he was not necessarily wholly subservient to her.

When referring to his response to the queen's commands he stated glibly, "I never deny; I never contradict; I sometimes forget."[6] While never openly disagreeing with his sovereign, he was often disobedient! Likewise many Christians pay lip service to God, but never follow through with their lives.

THE GIBEONITE DECEPTION

Joshua never hesitated to obey when he clearly knew God's will, but there were rare occasions when Joshua's carelessness cost him and his people. One such event involved the Gibeonites, a Canaanite kingdom. God steadfastly prohibited the Israelites from making any treaties with the inhabitants of Canaan (Ex. 23:31–33; Deut. 7:1–5; 20:16–18). God warned His people that the Canaanites would become a spiritual snare to them if they were permitted to live among them. Joshua was well aware of this and never knowingly allowed a Canaanite to escape his sword.

The Gibeonites knew they could not defeat Joshua. The stories of God's mighty acts terrified them (Josh. 9:9–11, 24). While other kingdoms braced themselves for war with the invaders, the Gibeonites resorted to deceit. They sent emissaries who pretended to be from a distant country. The men convinced Joshua and the Israelite elders to sign a peace treaty with them (Josh. 9:1–27).

When the Israelites discovered that Joshua and the elders had been duped, they were justifiably upset (Josh. 9:18). This is the only scriptural reference to complaints against Joshua's leadership. Joshua had not knowingly disobeyed God. But could he have avoided this calamity?

When Joshua met the Gibeonite messengers, they showed him moldy bread, aged wineskins, and dusty sandals and clothes they claimed were new when they began their journey (Josh. 9:12–13). It appeared they had traveled much farther than from within the land of Canaan.

Joshua and the elders carefully inspected the evidence before them and concluded they were hearing the truth. However, "they did not ask counsel of the Lord" (Josh. 9:14). This was Joshua's sin. Perhaps buoyed by recent successes, he and the elders chose to use their own judgment and they failed to seek God's direction. They knew better. God had closely walked with them every step so far.

"They did not ask counsel of the Lord."

Perhaps the elders assumed that while they were dependent on God to bring down fortress walls and to stop the flow of rivers, more straightforward tasks (such as interrogating foreign emissaries) were something they could handle on their own.

To Joshua's credit, he always learned from his mistakes. We do not read of another such lapse in his walk with God. As is the case with most sin, however, the consequences of even a momentary lapse can have lasting repercussions (2 Sam. 21:1–9). The Gibeonites remained in the promised land—a perpetual reminder of Joshua's oversight.

Spiritual leaders are usually highly capable people. Joshua certainly was a bright and talented man. The temptation for such people is to rely on their own instincts and to only "call God in" for the big stuff. But over and over again the Bible warns against relying on one's own best thinking. For example:

- Rebekah devised a plan to bless her youngest son, Jacob, and it caused her household to be torn asunder (Gen. 27).

- Samson attempted to fight the Philistines without God's power and he was captured and maimed (Judg. 16:18–21).

- King Solomon trusted in his internationally acclaimed wisdom rather than in God's word, so God raised up adversaries to oppose the disobedient king for the remainder of his reign (1 Kings 11:14, 23, 26).

- King Ahab thought he could trust in his army rather than in God and he was killed in battle (1 Kings 22:1–37).

Surely Jesus was speaking to every generation when He declared: "For without Me you can do nothing" (John 15:5). Wise leaders carefully consider what they are actually capable of accomplishing apart from God. The biblical answer, of course, is nothing.

CANAANITE SURVIVAL

Joshua's conquests were, on the whole, extremely extensive and successful. But there may have been another area where he was not as thorough as he should have been. While it appears that Joshua defeated many of his enemies, he did not defeat them all (Josh. 13:1–7). We read of his southern campaign:

> And at that time Joshua came and cut off the Anakim from the mountains: from Hebron, from Debir, from Anab, from all the mountains of Judah, and from all the mountains of Israel; Joshua utterly destroyed them with their cities. None of the Anakim were left in the land of the children of Israel; they remained only in Gaza, in Gath, and in Ashdod. So Joshua took the whole land, according to all that the LORD had said to Moses; and Joshua gave it as an inheritance to Israel according to their divisions by their tribes. Then the land rested from war. (Joshua 11:21–23)

The Anakim were reportedly gigantic people (Num. 13:32–33). These were the mighty warriors who had petrified ten of the twelve spies. Joshua, however, appears to have defeated most of them. None were left in the lands occupied by the Israelites (Josh. 11:22). Yet they still resided in the outlying cities of Gaza, Gath, and Ashdod. These were cities God intended for the Israelites to ultimately conquer and inhabit. In fact, there were numerous regions left unconquered after Joshua lay down his sword (Judg. 1:27–2:6; 3:1–6).

Apparently Joshua had subdued the major cities and enemy fortresses throughout Canaan but he left it to the individual tribes to complete the work of eradicating the enemy from the land. Most of the tribes failed to do this. The consequences were far reaching.

Joshua failed to capture the city of Gath where the legendary Anakim lived. Gath became a Philistine stronghold that brought tremendous grief to the Israelites for generations. A champion Philistine soldier came out of Gath to humiliate the Israelites. His name was Goliath (1 Sam. 17:4). Later, the Philistines killed the Israelites' first king, King Saul (1 Sam. 31). The inability of the Israelites to conquer the city of Gath as God intended cost their descendents dearly for many generations.

Joshua certainly was not willfully disobedient to God's command. He urged the people to complete the work he had begun. However, because Joshua's generation failed to completely remove the Canaanites from the land, the Israelites were soon tempted by the pagan practices and loose morals of their Canaanite neighbors, just as God had predicted (Judg. 2:11–15, 3:7). This would bring enormous suffering and grief to Israel until their disloyalty ultimately cost them four hundred years of turmoil during the period of the judges and later seventy years of exile in Babylon.

CONCLUSION

Oswald Chambers once said, "It is more and more impossible to me to have programs and plans because God alone has the plan, and our plans are only apt to hinder him, and make it necessary for him to break them up."[7] Joshua was not perfect in his walk with God. There were times when he failed to complete everything God instructed. Yet throughout his life, Joshua took God's instructions extremely seriously. Joshua saw God's word as wholly

OBEDIENCE THAT GOES THE DISTANCE

binding upon him. With Joshua there was no quarreling. There was no nego-
tiating. There was no delaying. There was no revising. There was only absolute
and immediate obedience. Such an attitude was the key to his success.

OBEDIENCE THAT GOES THE DISTANCE

- Joshua yielded to God.
- Joshua obeyed God.
- Joshua accepted hard assignments.
- Joshua's obedience was unflinching.
- Joshua occasionally blew it.

QUESTIONS FOR CONSIDERATION

1. When God speaks, what is your spontaneous reaction:
   submission or resistance?
2. Are you presently struggling under a difficult assignment? What
   might God want to teach you?
3. How are you currently suffering the consequences of your past
   disobedience to God?
4. What does your resistance to God's will indicate about your
   relationship with Him?

SIX

CHARACTER: THE FOUNDATION FOR LEADERSHIP

HIS BIRTH WAS SOMETHING OF A MIRACLE. Of the twelve children born into his family, seven died in infancy. His parents, never far from poverty, required him to forfeit his inheritance so they could avoid financial ruin. His military career initially flourished only to flounder when a new king ascended the throne. Despite his recognized courage and ability in warfare, the monarch deliberately snubbed him and appointed less-skilled men to command the royal troops.

Still in the prime of his life, he seemed destined to sit on a shelf and watch his life pass by as others did what he longed to do himself. The king was evidently determined to prevent him from ever enjoying success. His life reached its nadir when he was falsely accused of treason. He was sent to the Tower of London and ordered to stand trial for his life. Had his accusers not eventually confessed their duplicity, he may well have died a humiliating death on the scaffold, garnering hardly more than a footnote in the annals of British history.

The six years he spent in royal disfavor would appear to have been a tremendous waste of what historians now recognize was an enormous talent. But the years were not squandered. In fact, throughout the time John Churchill, later the Duke of Marlborough, suffered the displeasure of King William III, his character matured and developed.

His biographer and illustrious descendent, Winston Churchill, said: "Few features in Marlborough's long life are more remarkable than the manner in which he steadily grew in weight and influence through the whole of the six years when he was banished from favour and office."[1] While Marlborough had no control over his king or the political climate in which he lived, he was sovereign over what kind of person he would become.

Incredibly, though the king had shunned him and though he had never commanded an army, when England later faced an international crisis, Englishmen everywhere recognized him as the most gifted and respected leader among them. Marlborough would lead England's forces as well as many other European armies in a decade-long struggle against King Louis XIV and the seemingly invincible legions of France.

Marlborough gained such a commanding presence that Churchill notes: "His appearance, his serenity, his piercing eye, his gestures, the tone of his voice—nay, the beat of his heart—diffused a harmony upon all around him. Every word he spoke was decisive. Victory often depended upon whether he rode half a mile this way or that."[2]

The Duke of Marlborough led England into a state of preeminence among the world's great nations. He was always a force to be reckoned with. Despite the hardships of his childhood, despite the snub of his superiors, despite the attacks of his critics, despite the fierce opposition of his enemies, he had grown into an indomitable leader who would leave an enduring legacy to his nation and to world affairs.

CHARACTER: THE KEY TO SUCCESS

It seems somewhat unusual that the biblical account of a mighty general like Joshua makes no mention of his size or strength or appearance. In an age where brawn counted for a lot, Joshua's physical features seemed irrelevant. In God's kingdom such things don't matter; character does. People can only do so much to improve their physical and mental abilities, but the potential for character growth is limitless.

Big assignments require a certain maturity of character. Biblically, when

People can only do so much to improve their physical and mental abilities, but the potential for character growth is limitless.

God had an important task, he usually bypassed the most "obvious" candidates (according to the world's perspective). He chose a poor, unknown teenaged girl to bear the Messiah. He chose a simple shepherd boy to be Israel's greatest king. He called on an outspoken, impulsive fisherman to become an apostle.

The common denominator among all those God used mightily is character. That is not to say each of these people had "arrived" and attained perfection. But they were all willing for God to shape them and stretch them into the people He wanted for His assignments. That potential lay deep within—so deep that sometimes only God could see it—their character.

Joshua's case is somewhat unusual for a leader who is mentioned so often in the Bible. Invariably a spiritual leader, no matter how famous, will eventually reveal a character flaw. But Joshua doesn't. This doesn't mean he was sinless but that he had no character weakness significant enough for Scripture to mention.

- Noah was the only righteous man on earth, but he still became drunk with wine and disgraced himself (Gen. 9:21).

- Abraham was a man of faith, but he was also a liar (Gen. 12:11–13; 20:2).

- Abraham's son Isaac was a liar, and Isaac's son Jacob was a deceiver (Gen. 26:7; 27:19).

- Moses struggled with anger (Ex. 2:11–12; 32:19; Num. 20:1–13; Lev. 10:16).

- King Saul was jealous, and King David was adulterous (1 Sam. 18:7–9; 2 Sam. 11:4).

History's most celebrated leaders have been plagued by every besetting sin imaginable; these pages are not extensive enough to chronicle them. However, anger seems to be a common sin shared by many famous leaders.

Napoleon would lose his temper and usually regret it.[3] The wrath of Queen Elizabeth I was notorious. She would fly into a rage and punch her advisors or throw her slippers at their faces.

One of her attendants said, "When she smiled . . . it was a pure sunshine that everyone did choose to bask in if they could, but anon came a storm from a sudden gathering of clouds, and the thunder fell in wondrous manner all alike." A French ambassador said, "When I see her enraged against any person whatever, I wish myself in Calcutta, fearing her anger like death itself."[4]

Queen Victoria's acknowledged character weakness was anger. The diminutive queen, though less than five feet tall could strike fear into a great noble merely by the phrase, "We are not amused." Ponsonby, one of Victoria's advisors, wrote to his wife, "All, high and low, dread the chance of a disapproving nod—and yet you tell me that she has no power."[5]

CHARISMA OR CHARACTER?

What people do spontaneously or when no one is watching reveals their character. Likewise, what people do habitually reflects what lies within them. A leader's skills can temporarily mask a weak character, but eventually all leaders are revealed for who they really are. A charming, charismatic person may fool people for a time, but inevitably a lack of Christlike character becomes apparent (Matt. 7:15–20).

King Saul was Israel's first monarch. The Israelites craved someone who looked like the kings of other nations. They clamored for a leader who could carry himself with pomp and splendor like the world's great monarchs (1 Sam. 8:19–20). So God gave them a man who had all the qualities important to them. He was tall and physically impressive. He could act like a king and he demanded his people's respect.

After King Saul's coronation, his shallow character quickly showed itself. For one thing, he could be greedy (1 Sam. 15:9). He made harsh, unreasonable demands of his people. He was even prepared to execute his own son for disobeying his foolish orders (1 Sam. 14:44). Yet he showed no compunction in breaking God's laws (1 Sam. 13:13; 15:19).

As time wore on, Saul revealed a petty jealousy of anyone who threatened his position (1 Sam. 18:8). Though a king, Saul was even jealous of his servant (1 Sam. 18:12). Saul's character was marked by paranoia, self-pity, and cruel vengeance (1 Sam. 22:8, 17–18). Even when David twice spared his life, Saul's unrelenting hatred drove him to doggedly pursue David and his men (1 Sam. 24:16–22; 26:21–25).

Saul's life is a tragic illustration of the difference between charisma and character. He appeared impressive on the outside but the longer he ruled, the more obvious it became that his character was not robust enough to sustain his position.

It was said of Crassus, Julius Caesar's friend and rival, "All his difficulties arose because he set his sights too high. It was unfortunate that he was plagued by greed . . . nothing he did to further this ambition could make up for his essential mediocrity."[6] It is a dangerous venture to hold a position that is larger than your character.

Joshua's life exemplifies the qualities of a genuine leader. Joshua didn't obtain his position overnight as Saul did, but when he eventually achieved it, he was ready for it. Joshua never took on more than he could handle. His success never inflated his ego. He never seemed overwhelmed by his responsibilities. His character always matched the challenge that lay before him. When God chooses a leader He doesn't bypass character. He develops those He calls into people of moral strength. Then He uses them as His servants to build His kingdom.

When God chooses a leader He doesn't bypass character.

Unfortunately, churches often place more value on charisma than on character. They select pastors who look impressive and who make a good first impression, but they are later disappointed when their pastor's true character comes to light. Men and women are given important leadership roles because of their attractive appearance or prominent position or financial status rather than because of their close walk with God. It is not the godliest church members who clamor for positions and recognition. As a result they are often bypassed while people of lesser integrity assume roles that don't suit their character.

Was Joshua perfect when God chose him? Of course not. But he was willing for God to strengthen him and to work into him the godly qualities necessary for the enormous assignment of leading a nation. Saul, on the other hand, seems to have degenerated the longer he remained in power. His character simply couldn't handle the burden of leadership. Joshua paid the price to be the man God wanted him to be. Saul didn't earn his position, so he never developed the strength of character to maintain it.

CHARACTER: FORGED BY CRISIS

Winston Churchill once observed: "It is said that famous men are usually the product of an unhappy childhood."[7] One might assume Joshua's greatness came not just from the hardship of his early life but also from the challenges of a difficult adulthood. He was beset by one painful, disappointing experience after another.

He was born into slavery. It would seem he lost his parents at a relatively early age. He spent forty years in a wilderness because his colleagues lacked faith. He watched his spiritual leaders and heroes die one by one until only the grizzled Caleb remained. Even when Joshua was experiencing success as his nation's preeminent general, he was immersed in constant warfare and bloodshed. His was not an easy life.

Joshua could not pick and choose God's assignments for him. He had no control over what his fellow Israelites or his enemies would do. What Joshua could determine was how accessible to God his life would be. Regardless of whether God allowed Joshua to enter the promised land or not, Joshua could experience God working in his own life.

Whether or not Joshua ever saw the land of Canaan transformed into a dwelling place for God's people, he could experience God transforming his character into one that glorified God. A person's character is the sphere in which God delights to work. God receives glory through a godly character.

A strong character never happens overnight. It always involves more than simply gaining knowledge of God's Word. It takes living out the truth of God's Word in real-life situations.

A weak, underdeveloped character is no match for the spiritual magnitude of leading God's people. It is crucial for a leader that God builds his or her character. This always comes at a cost. Usually the process begins when the leader is young. Such was the case in both Moses' and Joshua's lives.

SUFFERING BUILDS CHARACTER

History is replete with examples of people suffering during their youth and then using those painful experiences to build a robust and refined character. Historians rank Queen Elizabeth I as one of the greatest monarchs in English history. At three months of age she was sent to live apart from her parents. After her mother, Anne Boleyn, was beheaded by order of Elizabeth's father, Henry VIII, three-year-old Elizabeth was estranged from her father and rarely saw him.

> A weak, underdeveloped character is no match for the spiritual magnitude of leading God's people.

The reign of her older sister, "Bloody Mary," saw her imprisoned in the Tower of London, where she spent each day expecting the same grisly fate as her mother's at the executioner's block. When she was told she was the new queen, she sank to her knees and said: "This is the Lord's doing: it is marvelous in our eyes."[8] She often thanked God for "pulling me from the prison to the palace."[9] As the royal officials watched the twenty-five-year-old queen they could not foresee that she would enjoy one of the longest and most illustrious reigns in English history.

Ulysses Grant attended West Point military academy and, upon his graduation, proudly wore his uniform as he traveled through town. As he grandly paraded himself through the city of Cincinnati, a young boy mocked him. Later in the town of Bethel, a stable hand began imitating the young soldier, much to the merriment of the townspeople.

These early humiliating experiences, while not earth-shattering events, had such a profound effect on the future general's life that he later observed: "The conceit was knocked out of me."[10] Never again did Grant flaunt himself before people and he seemed loath to even wear his general's uniform if he could avoid doing so.

D. L. Moody was the fifth son of nine children. His father was a lovable man, but his addiction to whiskey prevented him from adequately providing for his extensive family. He died when Moody was only four, leaving his family bankrupt. Moody's mother, Betsey, gave birth to twins shortly after her husband's death. Four days after the births, her creditor, Richard Colton, approached her bedside and demanded payment of the farm's mortgage.

If this was not enough for the destitute family, Moody's oldest brother, Isaiah, ran away at age fifteen. Moody grew up with great responsibilities while receiving a meager education. By age seventeen, he left home to find work.[11] It would be these early hardships and the profound influence of his mother that God used as building blocks in fashioning the humble character of the greatest evangelist of his day.

Many of the character traits that run deepest are those that are driven in hardest. Hard times imprint themselves into a person's character. Trials either leave a scar of bitterness and cynicism, or they forge strength, humility, and compassion

The difference is wholly dependent upon how people respond to their life situations and more importantly, how they respond to God in the midst of those circumstances (Rom. 8:28). While no one but a masochist looks for opportunities to suffer, people who truly desire to be Christlike in every part of their lives will welcome whatever instrument God uses to make them so.

It was James who urged believers to "Count it all joy when you fall into various trials, knowing that the testing of your faith produces patience. But let patience have its perfect work, that you may be perfect and complete, lacking nothing" (James 1:2–4).

Joshua approached the challenging moments of his life with great faith and humble dependence on God. While hardships tempted many of his colleagues to forfeit their faith, Joshua grew to trust God more. The result was a sterling moral fiber that could stand firm in the face of temptation, fear, and doubt.

Trials either leave a scar of bitterness and cynicism, or they forge strength, humility and compassion.

CHARACTER: KEEPING YOUR WORD

Joshua was a man of his word. There was always a perfect match between his words and his actions. When he sent two spies to reconnoiter Jericho, the local authorities attempted to arrest them. Only the intervention of Rahab, the harlot, saved their lives (Josh. 2:1–24). In response to her kindness, the two spies promised to spare her and any of her family members who gathered in her home during the upcoming attack.

On the day of the assault, Joshua saw to it that this promise was honored (Josh. 6:17, 22–25). In Joshua's day, men did not normally enter into agreements with women. Certainly a promise to a prostitute could have been excused or forgotten during the intensity of battle. Joshua had not even made the promise himself, but he was diligent to keep it.

When Joshua and the elders were duped by the Gibeonites, they promised to enter a peace treaty with them. After the Israelites discovered the deception, their first impulse was to immediately destroy their clever enemy. Nevertheless, Joshua and the elders chose to honor their word (Josh. 9:17–19). Even though they had been outmaneuvered, Joshua and his colleagues believed they would be accountable to God for not keeping their promise. Such fidelity to one's word is truly remarkable.

Before the American Civil War, Ulysses Grant plummeted to the depths of poverty and shame. During this humiliating period in his life, he had a memorable encounter. Several officers from Grant's former unit in the army, including Major Longstreet, who had been best man at Grant's wedding, were in St. Louis. They wanted to play cards together at the Planters Hotel and being short one player, they sent out Captain Edmund Holloway to conscript another hand. He brought Grant back with him.

Longstreet was immediately saddened by the pitiful condition to which his friend had been reduced since his disgraceful discharge from the military. The men had an enjoyable round of cards and then Grant parted company with them. Longstreet records:

> The next day I was walking in front of the Planters, when I found myself face
> to face again with Grant who, placing in the palm of my hand a five dollar

gold piece, insisted that I should take it in payment of a debt of honor over fifteen years old. I peremptorily declined to take it, alleging that he was out of the service and more in need of it than I. "You must take it," said he. "I cannot live with anything in my possession which is not mine." Seeing his determination in the man's face, and in order to save him mortification, I took the money, and shaking hands we parted.[12]

Grant had given his word and even dire poverty would not excuse him from fulfilling it.

Joshua's stalwart adherence to his word brought him great respect. When Joshua had Achan put to death for disobeying God, he vowed to do the same to the next person caught violating God's commands. Everyone knew he meant it. Joshua never deceived them. He never retracted his words. To know what Joshua said was to know what he would do. This gave his followers tremendous confidence.

CARELESS PROMISES REDUCE INFLUENCE

A sure way for a leader to forfeit his influence with followers is to make careless promises. Some leaders enter organizations effusing promises to all who listen. Every good idea that enters their head becomes a promise from their lips. Yet as quickly as the oaths are out of their mouths they are just as readily forgotten. Followers soon recognize such people and grow to disregard everything they say.

Some people in leadership positions constantly make pronouncements about things but they have no intention of acting on them. Richard Nixon often did this while he was president. After a rough landing in Air Force One at the beginning of his presidency, Nixon declared: "That's it! No more landing at airports!"[13]

In moments of frustration, the president would shout, "I want everyone fired, I mean it this time."[14] Of course when leaders constantly make such rash statements, they cease to be taken seriously.

Some leaders repeatedly threaten to resign if they do not get their way, but they never follow through. Others promise to listen to any suggestion, but they become angry and defensive when critiqued. Others promise to faithfully support their colleagues but they disappear when the pressure is on.

Some of the most haphazard vows made are those offered to God. It is sobering to consider how many empty promises God hears from well-intentioned but insincere people. Scripture warns of the gravity of not keeping vows made to God (Eccl. 5:2–5). Leaders' words are their currency but those words are worthless unless they are backed by action.

> A sure way for a leader to forfeit his influence with followers is to make careless promises.

CHARACTER: KEEPING YOUR HEAD

Certainly no Israelite was more highly esteemed in his day than Joshua. Scripture indicates, "The Lord exalted Joshua in the sight of all Israel; and they feared him, as they had feared Moses, all the days of his life . . . so the Lord was with Joshua, and his fame spread throughout all the country" (Josh. 4:14; 6:27).

Surely such honor from God and such respect by the people would have provided ample opportunity for Joshua to gain a high opinion of himself. Yet despite reaching the pinnacle of military and political power, Joshua never allowed his success to go to his head. He remained God's faithful servant throughout his life.

Joshua was meticulous in giving God the credit for his success. He continually reminded people that it was not his military stratagems or brilliant feats on the battlefield that brought victory. Rather he steadfastly pointed to God's presence as the key:

> And Joshua said to the people, "Sanctify yourselves, for tomorrow the LORD will do wonders among you." (Josh. 3:5)

> For the LORD your God dried up the waters of the Jordan before you until you had crossed over, as the LORD your God did to the Red Sea, which He dried up before us until we had crossed over. (Josh. 4:23)

> You have seen all that the LORD your God has done to all these nations because of you, for the LORD your God is He who has fought for you. (Josh. 23:3)

> For the LORD our God is He who brought us and our fathers up out of the land of Egypt, from the house of bondage, who did those great signs in our sight, and preserved us in all the way that we went and among all the people through whom we passed. (Josh. 24:17)

Joshua could easily have assumed he was at least *partially* responsible for the Israelite's dramatic success, but he didn't. Today's Christian leaders can struggle with how to view their careers. Successful businesspeople who have amassed fortunes through wise business practices and prudent investments can assume that, while God has blessed them (whatever that means), their success came by their own diligence and shrewdness. Pastors of growing churches can conclude that the development of their churches is due in large part to their own leadership skills and the passionate vision they have pursued for their congregations.

However, Joshua understood that ultimately, nothing he did had significance unless God affirmed it. God gave Joshua every skill and every strategy he brought to the battlefield, because God was the author of Joshua's very life.

Joshua knew he was always just one stray arrow or one sudden sword thrust away from abruptly ending his brilliant leadership career. One rebellion or one murderous traitor and Joshua's life could end in agony. Julius Caesar could not be defeated on the battlefield but he miscalculated his good friend Brutus and Brutus's twenty-two fellow assassins.

Alexander the Great conquered the known world but fell victim to disease in the prime of his life. Dying in the luxurious palace of Nebuchadnezzar, he was reminded that even the greatest conquerors in history have lived at the pleasure and whim of almighty God. Napoleon Bonaparte was the most famous emperor of his age but he was just one Waterloo away from exile and ruin.

HUMBLE DESPITE SUCCESS

It's a refreshing thing to witness leaders who remain humble despite their success. It has been said of the Duke of Marlborough: "He yielded neither to success nor exhaustion."[15] His biographer notes: "It is Marlborough's true glory that the higher his fortunes, the higher rose his virtue."[16]

Around 1814, the Duke of Wellington, the famed victor of Waterloo, was attending a ball at the fashionable Almack's club. Rather than the prescribed knee breeches and silk stockings, he inadvertently wore black trousers. Mr. Willis met the renowned duke at the door and stodgily informed him, "Your Grace cannot be admitted in trousers." The duke was the most famous man in England; he'd saved his country. Yet he humbly turned around and departed.[17]

On another occasion when he was at the height of his popularity as prime minister, he was riding in his carriage to Buckingham Palace. Upon entering Hyde Park he was informed that no carriages were currently being allowed through. The officer who stopped Wellington, upon realizing whom he was detaining, hurriedly explained that the rule surely did not apply to him. However, Wellington dutifully ordered his carriage to make a detour, explaining that he would follow the rules just like everyone else.[18]

Alexander Stephens, vice president of the Confederacy, observed of Robert E. Lee, "What I had seen General Lee to be at first—child-like in simplicity and unselfish in character—he remained, unspoiled by praise and success."[19] General Lee's victorious antagonist Ulysses Grant humbly observed of his own success: "'Man proposes and God disposes.' There are but few important events in the affairs of men brought about by their own choice."[20] These accomplished leaders managed to keep their success in proper perspective.

Joshua's dismal experience at the city of Ai was proof enough, if he needed any, that God's presence was everything. The moment God withdrew His presence from the previously undefeated Israelite forces, their army was turned back in a rout.

We counsel numerous Christian CEOs of large corporations. When we ask why they have achieved so much, many give a sober reply. They cannot always explain why they have enjoyed such prosperity. They have friends who've worked as hard and who have more talent, yet have not fared as well.

It becomes apparent that despite their strenuous efforts, their success has caught them by surprise. Often they conclude God must want to use them for some purpose and that's why He has allowed them to succeed. We know many CEOs and business owners who take their faith seriously and make significant sacrifices so that their companies honor God.

A number of Christian business owners have refused to downsize their companies when the economy plummeted, even though it would have been seen as a prudent step to take. As a result, they have spared hundreds of families from financial hardship.

The founder of a software company established a charitable foundation with a portion of his earnings and used it to promote Christian education around the world. A businesswoman used her personal resources to found and fund an orphanage in an impoverished region in Asia. Owners of professional sports teams have hired chaplains to help players find Christ and then to disciple them. Some CEOs give of their personal wealth to provide aid to the poor or to sponsor mission projects such as building houses for impoverished families. Others have used their influential positions to pressure television networks to remove morally offensive advertisements during family viewing hours.

Some Christian business leaders use their private jets to transport church leaders to ministry events. Many offer their vacation properties as places of restful retreat for overwhelmed Christian ministers and their families. Some use their wealth to start up Christian enterprises or to have Christian materials published and distributed.

Many CEOs generously invest company resources to help employees further their education and skill development. Some business owners invest their resources into providing Christian counseling to employees. Some corporate executives use their access to world leaders as an opportunity to share the gospel with the world's most powerful people.

They understand that their success is really God's success.

The list of ways Christian business leaders have invested their influence and wealth into the kingdom of God seems endless. These practices do not always seem to make the best business sense, but these Christian leaders know it is one way God is using them to build *His* kingdom.

These leaders (and we haven't named them) don't do this to win accolades, but we can assure you that throughout the corporate world, there are many fine Christian leaders who are making a profound difference upon those they lead. They are doing it because they understand that their success is really God's success.

When Christian business leaders assume they are the authors of their own success, they lack a sense of divine stewardship. They focus on amassing their fortunes rather than on building God's kingdom. They achieve personal glory rather than glorifying God. They write "how to" books so that people can copy their success, but they don't point people to God.

> God does not take second place in anyone's life. God does not receive glory by making our plans succeed, but by accomplishing His will.

Some Christian businesspeople live the first half of their lives feverishly gaining fame and fortune by their own efforts. Then, once they have achieved their goals and obtained a comfortable level of wealth, they turn to God and unconvincingly give the "glory" to God for their accomplishments. Biblically, however, this does not honor God. This is merely second-hand glory and God does not take second place in anyone's life. God does not receive glory by making *our* plans succeed, but by accomplishing *His* will. Joshua understood this. From the outset of his military career until his retirement speech, Joshua regularly and sincerely gave all the glory to God for his success. In his mind, it *was* God's success.

THE TEST OF SUCCESS

It has been said that George Washington was a "veritable virtuoso of exits."[21] Each time Washington completed the assignment his nation gave him, he retired. Some people feared that once elected president of the United States, Washington would rule for life as a quasi-king.

John Adams once commented on Washington's enormous influence: "If he were not really one of the best intentioned men in the world, he might be a very dangerous one."[22] Yet after two terms in office, Washington retired and allowed the fledgling democratic process to reach maturity under the next generation of leaders.

Joseph Ellis commented that Washington "became the supreme example of the leader who could be trusted with power because he was so ready to give it up."[23] Washington understood that he had been entrusted with a great responsibility but that it was a stewardship, not a right.

A sure way to tell what people are made of is to examine what they do with success and the accompanying power and fame it brings. Joshua could have brokered his exalted position to benefit himself financially, but he never abused the office God entrusted to him. After accomplishing God's assignment, he voluntarily stepped down and out of the limelight.

Joshua did not need a prestigious job to feel significant. He did not derive his self-worth from the attention and praise of others. He did not nurse feelings of entitlement as a result of his labors. His relationship with God gave him more than enough reason to feel satisfied.

It is said of Napoleon Bonaparte and his family, "He showered on them and their spouses principalities and kingdoms, but all were lost, and all his siblings met misfortune or underwent long years in exile."[24] Napoleon's biographer explains much of his corrupt behavior: "He emerged from a political background where a man's word meant nothing, honor was dead, and murder was routine."[25]

As Alexander the Great systematically subdued his enemies, his demands of the people increased proportionately. Near the close of his life Alexander requested that the Greek city-states grant him divine recognition as a son of either the god Zeus or Amnon.[26]

Once while Alexander was being transported in a small boat, the royal diadem fell from his head into the sea. A diligent sailor leaped into the water and retrieved it for his king. To show his gratitude, Alexander gave the sailor a talent of gold. Then he had him executed for having dared to place the royal crown upon his head while he swam back to the boat![27]

As Julius Caesar reached the pinnacle of his powers, he discarded personal restraint like an old toga. He showered himself with accolades and tributes. He directed a feast to be held in which twenty-two thousand people sat and ate in his honor. Senators swore elaborate oaths to protect his life. His decrees were dutifully pre-approved by the docile senate before he even announced them.

Four yearly games were held in his name. His image was marched in procession as if he were a god. A gable was built on to his house mimicking a temple. Such extravagance showered upon one man was unheard of even in an age when people routinely indulged in excess.[28] Caesar became so confident and arrogant that he dismissed his bodyguard, thus bringing about his doom.

Joshua was surrounded by success and power. Kings paid homage to him. Yet Joshua kept his feet on the ground and never allowed his success to go to his head.

CHARACTER: CONSIDERING OTHERS

It has been said "no man is a hero to his valet." Peruse the biography section of a bookstore and notice how many former employees and attendants enthusiastically reveal the scandalous side of their famous former employers. Many widely acclaimed heroes and admired leaders are not looked upon so highly by those who must work with them on a daily basis.

God exalted Joshua before his people. It would have been easy for him to abuse this influence over others. Joshua never believed that because he had accomplished much for his people he was entitled to any special favors or honors. There is no evidence that Joshua's success desensitized him to those he led. There is no record of Joshua being self-centered. By all accounts Joshua's people willingly followed him anywhere and faced any enemy.

There is no evidence that Joshua's success desensitized him to those he led.

When Joshua was dividing the promised land among the tribes and families of Israel, he had everyone else receive their inheritance before he was finally given his own plot (Josh. 19:49–51). No one had worked harder or played a more decisive role in the Israelites' success than Joshua. But he was the last to benefit personally from his own victories and he received no more than anyone else. Obviously Joshua was a humble man of integrity who knew who he was and to whom he was accountable.

GREAT LEADERS ARE SENSITIVE TO NEEDS

A mark of great leaders is how sensitive they are to the needs of those they lead. The Duke of Marlborough was famous among his men for ensuring their well-being. One of his corporals wrote, "His attention and care . . . was over us all." His biographer said:

> Always patiently and thoroughly examining the conditions on the front of the army, unwearied by ten campaigns, burdened by no sense of his own importance, undiscouraged by the malice of his enemies at home, he performed to the very end most faithfully and vigilantly the daily duty of a soldier. It was through this rule of conduct that he earned from the rank and file the nickname, "the Old Corporal."[29]

Admiral Nelson was wounded during his great naval victory at the Bay of Aboukir and brought below deck for medical attention. When the ship's surgeon noticed the admiral, he turned away from the other wounded sailors he was tending. "No, I will take my turn with my brave fellows," said Nelson.[30] This and other acts of respect he showed his men incited Nelson's sailors to perform valiantly wherever they served with him.

A mark of great leaders is how sensitive they are to the needs of those they lead.

Robert E. Lee's son fought in his father's army. He observed of his father: "In common with all his soldiers, I felt that he was ever near, that he could be entirely trusted with the care of us, that he would not fail us, that it would all end well. The feeling of trust that we had in him was simply sublime . . . it never occurred to me, and to thousands and thousands like me, that there was any occasion for uneasiness."[31] It is not surprising that Lee's men fought gallantly whenever he led them.

After a bitterly fought encounter at the battle of Chattanooga, the Union

❦❦❦❦❦❦❦❦❦❦

Humility doesn't demand respect nor pursue revenge; humility only seeks a "well done" from the Lord.

❦❦❦❦❦❦❦❦❦❦

forces were processing the numerous Confederate prisoners they had captured during their victory. The parade of disheveled prisoners was halted to allow several Union generals and their staffs to ride by. As they rode past, they smugly looked upon the new prisoners with disdain.

One Confederate prisoner later recalled: "When General Grant reached the line of ragged, filthy, bloody, despairing prisoners strung out on each side of the bridge, he lifted his hat and held it over his head until he passed the last man of that living funeral cortege. He was the only officer in that whole train who recognized us as being on the face of the earth."[32] At the close of the war, it was Grant who threatened to resign his post if Robert E. Lee and his officers were tried for treason. He probably saved them from the gallows.[33]

Great leaders even treat their enemies with dignity and grace. Spiritual leaders also conduct themselves with humility. Humility doesn't demand respect nor pursue revenge; humility only seeks a "well done" from the Lord.

CHARACTER: ACCOUNTABLE TO GOD

The Duke of Marlborough was undefeatable on the battlefield for ten years of intense military campaigns in Europe. He directed armies of 100,000 soldiers through intricate and complicated maneuvers. He regularly met with the most powerful monarchs and rulers in the world. He led his troops in gallant charges against the enemy, but he had his limitations.

When his wife Sarah fell into disfavor with Queen Anne and was removed from her station as a lady-in-waiting, Marlborough returned to England and sought an audience with his queen. Despite being the greatest military man in the world at the time, he knelt before the monarch and begged on behalf of his wife.[34] Such humility from a decorated hero seemed startling. Yet the embattled duke understood that all his powers were his by gift of his sovereign. As his biographer said: "He might be the greatest of servants. He could be no more."[35]

118

Having a Christlike character is possible for every believer; God can do a transforming work in any person who is willing to let Him. But He leaves the choice to us. At the close of his life, Joshua urged the Israelites to "hold fast to the LORD" (Josh. 23:8). Joshua had spent a lifetime choosing God's way. Sometimes it meant risking his reputation. God often told him to do things that went against commonly accepted military and administrative opinion. Imagine announcing to your military officers God's plan for taking down the walls of Jericho! Joshua often faced the prospect of ridicule and second-guessing from those he led, yet he chose to cling to the Lord.

Joshua challenged the people to "choose for yourselves this day whom you will serve." Then he declared his own allegiance, and his words have become a mantra for believers ever since, "As for me and my house, we will serve the LORD" (Josh. 24:15).

Every person has the same option. It makes no difference whether one has been raised in a Christian environment or in an atheist household, whether a person is highly educated or illiterate, wealthy or destitute; choosing to obey God is a conscious decision every person has to regularly make.

Joshua clarified why he was so careful to obey God: "He is a holy God. He is a jealous God . . . If you forsake the LORD and serve foreign gods, then He will turn and do you harm and consume you, after He has done you good" (Josh. 24:19–20). Joshua knew he could not serve a holy God with an unholy life. Knowing what God was like gave Joshua the proper perspective to dutifully serve his Lord.

It wasn't a question of feelings or rights or preferences. It was a matter of reverence. Out of his awe for God grew a keen sense of accountability. Joshua realized God would discipline him if he abandoned His divine covenant. Knowing this, Joshua's only option was to completely submit himself to God. At the root of Joshua's faithfulness was a healthy fear of the LORD. He exhorted his people: "Fear the LORD, serve Him in sincerity and in truth" (Josh. 24:14).

> **It wasn't a question of feelings or rights or preferences. It was a matter of reverence.**

Queen Elizabeth I said, "We princes are set on stages, in the sight and view of all the world. It behooveth us to be careful that our proceedings be just and honorable."[36] Without exception, great spiritual leaders have a profound sense of accountability.

Without exception, great spiritual leaders have a profound sense of accountability.

They are guided by the realization that no matter how highly esteemed they are by people in this life, one day they will stand before almighty God. They will be face-to-face with their Creator and their life will be completely exposed for what it is, merits and faults alike. This truth terrified the apostle Paul. He knew full well the "terror of the Lord." He was constantly aware that serving God was serious business:

Therefore we make it our aim, whether present or absent, to be well pleasing to Him. For we must all appear before the judgment seat of Christ, that each one may receive the things done in the body, according to what he has done, whether good or bad. Knowing, therefore, the terror of the Lord, we persuade men; but we are well known to God. (2 Corinthians 5:9–11)

Tragically, many Christian leaders today are devoid of a profound sense of reverence for God. Today's Christian culture so emphasizes God's unmerited love, that to mention God's holiness and judgment is considered poor taste. Yet the writer of Proverbs urges wise people to maintain a palpable fear and reverence for God:

Then you will understand the fear of the LORD,
And find the knowledge of God. (Proverbs 2:5)

Do not be wise in your own eyes;
Fear the LORD and depart from evil. (Proverbs 3:7)

The fear of the LORD prolongs days,
But the years of the wicked will be shortened. (Proverbs 10:27)

The fear of the LORD leads to life,
And he who has it will abide in satisfaction;
He will not be visited with evil. (Proverbs 19:23)

It is impossible to fear God and yet tolerate sin in your life. Sin takes on an entirely different look when you are keenly aware you will one day give an account for it! God declares Himself to be a jealous God. This truth should profoundly impact those who follow Him. It is incredible that almighty God cares what His creatures do or believe. It is a costly mistake for people to assume God is either too distant to know what they are doing or too far removed in majesty to care about their loyalty or affections.

Joshua, the inveterate warrior, understood that God coveted his allegiance. God would not look the other way if Joshua betrayed Him. God would never be satisfied with the crumbs that fell from the plate of Joshua's affections. Joshua urged people to either wholeheartedly follow God or else to reject Him. He discouraged them from trying to follow God in a lackadaisical fashion. This, God would never accept (Josh. 24:19–20).

> **It is impossible to fear God and yet tolerate sin in your life.**

CONCLUSION

There are no shortcuts to success with God. God will systematically and thoroughly work *in* you as He works *through* you. Because God is seeking to do far more through your life than you could imagine, He is constantly stretching you and molding you and fashioning your character to be like Christ's. The deeper your walk with God, the more Christlike your character will be. Wholly submitting yourself to God's will is the surest way to have a life God is pleased to use for His purposes.

CHARACTER: THE FOUNDATION OF LEADERSHIP

- Character: The Key to Success
- Character: Forged by Crisis
- Character: Keeping Your Word

- Character: Keeping Your Head
- Character: Considering Others
- Character: Accountable to God

QUESTIONS FOR CONSIDERATION

1. What key events in your life have shaped you to be the person you are? Are there any events or crises in your life you need to ask God to process with you?

2. What aspects of your character do you feel are displeasing to God? What is God doing in you to change your character? What are you doing?

3. Are you known as a person who keeps your word? Why or why not?

4. Have you inadvertently taken the credit for your leadership success? How can you change that?

5. Do people with whom you work believe you care about them? Do you tend to use people or bless them?

6. Do you often consider the fact that one day you will give a full accounting to God for how you led others? What do you anticipate that time will be like?

SEVEN

FAITH THAT
BRINGS WALLS DOWN

THEIR MARRIAGE BEGAN with a mutual eagerness to serve together on the mission field. Just two weeks after their wedding, they enthusiastically set sail on a 114-day journey to Calcutta, India. But their romantic notions of mission work evaporated upon their arrival. International conflicts prevented them from remaining in India and forced them to seek an alternate mission field.

Eventually they arrived in Burma, one of the most dangerous and oppressive places in the world. Missionaries sharing the gospel in that spiritually darkened country risked such brutal punishments as crucifixion, beheading, and having molten lead poured down their throats. During their early travels, their first child died while they were at sea. The couple's second child, Roger, died at six months of age. They waited two years before receiving their first mail. Their first convert was baptized seven years after they had left home for the mission field.

Then their disheartening situation grew unbearably worse. Armed police burst into their home, carried the husband away and locked him in a high security prison aptly dubbed the "Death House." Over fifty wretched prisoners were crammed into the dark, putrid, rat-infested quarters.

At night a bamboo pole would be lowered from the ceiling and pushed through the shackles on the prisoners' legs. Then the pole would be raised until only the prisoners' shoulders still touched the ground. The captives would hang upside down all night while the swarming insects feasted on their bloodied and bruised feet.

Each afternoon promptly at three o'clock, two guards would enter the cell and choose two prisoners for execution. Daily the prisoners waited to see whose turn it was to die. As they grimly watched two of their companions hauled away it was small comfort knowing they now had at least twenty-four more hours to live.

The missionary's daughter, Maria, was born while he languished in captivity. His wife contracted a severe case of dysentery and could not feed her baby. They had to bribe the prison warden to release the father from jail under guard each day so he could take his starving infant from house to house begging nursing mothers to spare some milk. At this desperate time in their lives, they had only seen eighteen converts in the twelve years they had served in Burma.[1]

No one could have blamed Adoniram and Nancy Judson had they lost hope. Yet they clung to the knowledge God had called them to share the good news of Jesus Christ with the Burmese people. Every circumstance implied failure and hopelessness, but they steadfastly trusted God to provide for them. Their faith was not misplaced; God did bring Adoniram release from prison and He gave them a fruitful ministry among the Burmese people. The Judson's story motivated a generation of Americans and scores of people responded to God's call into missions. All over the world were missionaries inspired by the faith the Judsons displayed in the face of a hopeless situation.

History's greatest saints have been ordinary people who held tenaciously to God's Word no matter what they encountered.

Scripture says, "Faith is the substance of things hoped for, the evidence of things not seen . . . But without faith it is impossible to please Him" (Heb. 11:1, 6). Faith means trusting God regardless of your circumstances. Faith means looking beyond the current situation and believing God will keep His promises. History's greatest saints have been ordinary people who held tenaciously to God's Word no matter what they encountered. God profoundly rewards those who put their faith in Him and leave it there.

Joshua's life was characterized by indomitable faith. He did not base his trust on life events but on his firsthand knowledge of God. Joshua's unshakable confidence in God becomes obvious as you examine the way he lived his life.

FAITH THAT STANDS FIRM

Leading followers is one thing. Leading leaders is another. When spies were needed to investigate Canaan each of the twelve tribes chose a prominent leader to represent them. Joshua was honored to be among them (Num. 13:2). Modern Bible teachers sometimes portray ten of these men as cowardly wimps. This is unquestionably too harsh. Each of these soldiers had risen to the apex of leadership in his tribe. Out of tribes consisting of tens of thousands, each was perceived as a strong, dominant leader. These men were respected. They were trusted. They had already proven themselves to be capable leaders, so when they spoke, people listened.

This band of spies spent forty days together while surveying Canaan. They traveled together; they ate their meals together; they hid from enemy patrols together. At night they took turns standing watch to protect each other. They undoubtedly had strong personalities and fervent opinions. Joshua may have been one of the youngest men on this dangerous mission. Day after day Joshua would have listened to his persuasive comrades vehemently argue their views about the feasibility of conquering Canaan.

Leading followers is one thing. Leading leaders is another.

When the group returned to report to their kinsmen, it was a pivotal moment in Israel's history. Ten of the spies began by describing a fertile and prosperous land, rich in resources. Then their account turned negative. They spoke of fierce giants and fortified cities (Num. 13:28–29, 31–33). These reputable men were doing exactly what they had been asked to do—reporting on what they saw.

As these eloquent spokesmen warmed to their subject, the people grew increasingly terrified. Obviously they were convincing. No one from the crowd challenged their opinion. No one questioned their information. No one charged them with cowardice. The testimony from such respected leaders sent an entire nation into a state of unrestrained pandemonium. Even Moses and Aaron fell on their faces before the people. Then it was Joshua's turn.

What was Joshua to do? These men were passionate. They were convincing. They had the nation's attention and their trust. To speak out against such popular leaders would take enormous courage. Besides, Joshua could not dispute the facts. There *were* fierce enemies. There *were* strong, fortified cities.

Joshua and the ten reluctant spies were looking at the same situation, but from different perspectives. Here is the report Joshua and Caleb gave:

> The land we passed through to spy out is an exceedingly good land. If the LORD delights in us, then He will bring us into this land and give it to us, "a land which flows with milk and honey." Only do not rebel against the LORD, nor fear the people of the land, for they are our bread; their protection has departed from them, and the LORD is with us. Do not fear them. (Numbers 14:7–9)

It was not a popular opinion to be shared at that moment! In fact, the people prepared to stone Joshua and Caleb to silence them (Num. 14:10). How much courage does it take to look in the faces of thousands of terrified people and tell them their viewpoint is wrong—that their fear is misplaced? What temerity is required to publicly disagree with ten of the nation's most trusted leaders? What kind of character is required to face a hostile and murderous mob, yet to tenaciously hold firm to one's convictions?

Joshua had faith. He knew God. He knew regardless of his enemies' size or strength, and no matter how weak he felt, with God all things were possible. It wasn't a matter of what Joshua did *not* know. His faith was based on what he *did* know. At this point Joshua faced a number of unknowns: He had no idea how many enemy soldiers his army would face. He could not anticipate his opponents' resources and alliances. Neither was he aware of God's plan to hold the sun in its place or to topple city walls. But he knew God, and everything he knew about God assured him he had nothing to fear.

Joshua's faith was not based on public opinion or on his own resources. It came out of his experiential knowledge of God. It was not a "blind faith" but faith based on his personal experience with God. After all, had God not already delivered them from Egypt and brought them safely to this moment? All twelve spies had the same evidence. But Joshua had a practical faith in God and this made all the difference.

> **It wasn't a matter of what Joshua did not know. His faith was based on what he did know.**

Hudson Taylor prayed every day over a map of China. His heart was heavily burdened for the millions of Chinese people who had never heard the gospel.

He carefully read God's Word and he knew God wanted him to claim that vast, populous region of the world for Christ. In light of Taylor's circumstances, such a feat was clearly impossible. For one thing, Taylor had no financial backing from any mission agency. There was no organization in China to coordinate the enterprise. As of yet, he knew of no other missionaries willing to serve with him.

Thoughts of evangelizing China to the extent God was leading him appeared ludicrous. Yet Taylor knew God had spoken. And he was convinced God would provide. Taylor was later asked about the mighty work God did through him in China. He said, "I often think that God must have been looking for someone small enough and weak enough for Him to use, and that He found me."[2]

Taylor always assumed God's presence and God's promises were more than enough to override any circumstances he faced. At one point his mission treasurer informed him they only had twenty-five-cents left in their account. Taylor joyfully replied, "Twenty-five cents . . . plus all the promises of God! Why, one felt as rich as Croesus!"[3]

Centuries before Taylor's day, Joshua had the same attitude. As long as he had received a promise from God, there was no reason to fret over the details.

God would provide. He chose to focus on God and His word rather than on the problems and the unknowns. Even when obstacles immobilized most of the people around him Joshua was motivated by the God he knew. That is not to imply a careless disregard for the difficult task ahead. Joshua was a skilled and competent leader in every respect.

FAITH: ONE STEP AT A TIME

> **Even when obstacles immobilized most of the people around him Joshua was motivated by the God he knew.**

The first logistical problem Joshua faced was the Jordan River. It was a formidable barrier, especially during flood season when the melting snows from the northern mountains could expand the floodplain up to a mile wide. During that time the flowing waters were transformed into a raging torrent. It would be an organizational nightmare to transport the supplies and equipment for an entire nation across the swollen river. God had previously performed a great miracle during Moses' leadership when He parted the Red Sea. The people had not yet seen if God would work as powerfully through Joshua. God parted a sea for Moses; would He stem a river's flow for Joshua?

We are not told if Joshua's faith wavered during his first big test, but his conduct indicates a steadfast trust in God:

So Joshua said to the children of Israel, "Come here, and hear the words of the LORD your God." And Joshua said, "By this you shall know that the living God is among you, and that He will without fail drive out from before you the Canaanites and the Hittites and the Hivites and the Perizzites and the Girgashites and the Amorites and the Jebusites: Behold, the ark of the covenant of the Lord of all the earth is crossing over before you into the Jordan. Now therefore, take for yourselves twelve men from the tribes of Israel, one man from every tribe. And it shall come to pass, as soon as the soles of the feet of the priests who bear the ark of the LORD, the Lord of all the earth, shall rest in the waters of the Jordan, that the waters of the Jordan shall be cut off, the waters that come down from upstream, and they shall stand as a heap." So it was, when the people set out from their camp to cross over the Jordan, with the priests bearing the ark of the covenant before the people, and as those who bore the ark came to the Jordan, and the feet of the priests who bore the ark dipped in the edge of the water (for the Jordan over-flows all its banks during the whole time of harvest), that the waters which came down from upstream stood still, and rose in a heap very far away at Adam, the city that is beside Zaretan. So the waters that went down into the Sea of the Arabah, the Salt Sea, failed, and were cut off; and the people crossed over opposite Jericho. Then the priests who bore the ark of the covenant of the LORD stood firm on dry ground in the midst of the Jordan; and all Israel crossed over on dry ground, until all the people had crossed completely over the Jordan. (Joshua 3:9–17)

How much faith does it take to gather an entire nation, have them pack up all their belongings and march them headlong into a raging river? Moses could at least stand still and watch the waters of the Red Sea divide before him (Ex. 14:21). But Joshua was commanded to march directly into the river; the only indication it would miraculously subside was God's promise that it would.

Only when the priests' toes entered the swirling waters did the river's flow cease. God could have parted the river the night before or He could have stopped the waters moments before the Israelites arrived. But He chose to stretch their faith. The way God performed this miracle was a test of His people and it certainly proved Joshua's unwavering trust in Him.

By withholding His intervention until the last possible moment, God allowed His people to demonstrate their entrenched confidence in Him. A desperate situation became a moment of triumph for God's people. They could henceforth remember this day as a time when they stepped out in faith and God was there to walk with them.

GEORGE MÜLLER: PRAYER WARRIOR

One of history's most famous prayer warriors was George Müller of Bristol, England. With very few resources, but abundant confidence in God, he ran a large orphanage. He trusted God to feed and to meet the needs of hundreds of orphaned boys and girls. Often, however, God's provision arrived at the last possible moment. At times Müller and the children would prepare to eat a meal that did not yet exist. Yet he would pray and give thanks for what God was *going to* provide. Then a knock at the door would come and God's provision would arrive, just in time. Müller testified that, though God never failed to provide, He sometimes delayed His response to strengthen Müller's faith:

> Now observe how the Lord helped us! A lady from London brought a parcel with money and rented a room next door to the boys' Orphan House. This afternoon she brought me the money which amounted to three pounds two shillings and sixpence. We were at the point of selling these things which could be spared, but this morning I asked the Lord to provide for us in another way. The money had been near the Orphan Houses for several days without being given. That proved to me that it was in the heart of God from the beginning to help us. But because He delights in the prayers of His children, He allowed us to pray so long. Our tried faith made the answer much sweeter.[4]

Most Christians would readily claim to believe God provides. Not many are willing to live out that trust in God's provision. Müller not only preached and taught about God's love, he modeled his faith by living it. Imagine all the children sitting at the table and listening to their headmaster express heartfelt thanks for food that was not yet there!

Müller's faith is reminiscent of Joshua's. Joshua acted on God's word even when it appeared such trust could lead to disaster. Someone who has not heard God speak as Joshua and Müller have might consider their actions merely reckless abandon caused by misguided presumption upon God. Yet when you have a promise from God, stepping out in faith is the most logical and reasonable thing you can do. It is not presumptuous to step out in obedience when you have just heard God speak.

The reason more people do not see Jordan Rivers parting in their lives and ministries is because they waver at the riverbank. They want to be people of faith but they conclude it would be much easier if God would part the waters *before* they had to get their feet wet!

Too often Christians begin to step out in obedience but they lose their nerve. They decide if God wanted them to cross the river He would have already parted the waters. They interpret the unchanged waters as a "closed door." God must not want them to proceed or He would have given them an "open door."

> **The reason more people do not see Jordan Rivers parting in their lives and ministries is because they waver at the riverbank.**

But God may be testing their faith. Perhaps He is watching to see what they will do with a word from Him. Only God knows how many miracles spiritual leaders have missed because they turned away from the river just before God planned to part the waters.

FAITH FOR THE FUTURE

When you consider how enormous the task of conquering and inhabiting Canaan was, you realize how astounding God's promise to the Israelites was! He was giving them a beautiful, fertile land (Num. 34:1–12). Its expansive territory spanned from the lands east of the Jordan River all the way west to the Mediterranean Sea; from the northern region of Mount Hor to the southern wilderness of Zin. Canaan was home to numerous fortresses and fortified cities. It was a land whose current occupants would zealously resist the trespass of unwelcome intruders, yet God said the land already belonged to the Israelites!

After Joshua conquered the Canaanites, God specifically guided him in parceling out the land (Josh. 15–21). It is striking how meticulous God's instructions were. Bible scholars find the lists so detailed, several of the territories mentioned are unknown to modern historians. God is that way. He deals in specifics, not in generalities. His plan for His people was tailor-made down to the last detail. For the Israelites to settle for anything less would have been to accept less than God's specific will for them.

In some cases Joshua allotted to tribes land that had not yet even been fully conquered. Yet Joshua treated them as already taken, based on God's promise:

> So the LORD gave to Israel all the land of which He had sworn to give to their fathers, and they took possession of it and dwelt in it. The LORD gave them rest all around, according to all that He had sworn to their fathers. And not a man of all their enemies stood against them; the LORD delivered all their enemies into their hand. Not a word failed of any good thing which the LORD had spoken to the house of Israel. All came to pass. (Joshua 21:43–45)

Christians often share with us stories of how they received a clear word from God but allowed circumstances to sidetrack them from following through. Some have said God spoke to them as teenagers about eventually serving in international missions. But years went by and they never pursued the call. Now they are middle-aged and they wonder if God could still use their lives in some way on the mission field.

Parents have shared with us how God told them their child would one day serve the Lord in Christian ministry. But their child was not currently walking closely with the Lord, so the parents assumed God had retracted His promise.

God promises all believers that nothing can separate them from His love. But a serious illness develops and they assume God must not care about them anymore. We've spoken to one whom God directed to start a business and use its assets to support the Lord's work globally. Then logistical challenges and difficult labor issues captured the business leader's attention and the vision God gave was abandoned.

When God makes a promise, it is critical to keep it before you. Live your life in the full anticipation that one day you will see God's promises come to pass. Discover what God said to your parents or grandparents and keep that before you as well! (Isa. 55:10–11).

God made everything He had promised available to His people during Joshua's time. Yet, the Israelites never fully occupied the land God said He wanted to give them. Israel reached its largest size territorially under King David, yet by the following generation, under Solomon's reign, it began shrinking in size as the surrounding kingdoms seized its lands. The reality is that God's people never fully enjoyed all God had promised. God had much more in mind for His people than they ever received.

> **When God makes a promise, it is critical to keep it before you. Live your life in the full anticipation that one day you will see God's promises come to pass.**

Much of the book of Joshua presents a paradox. We read that God *gave* the land to the Israelites, and then we find they still had to *take* it using military force. When Joshua first assumed his leadership role he reminded the people of God's promise: "Remember the word which Moses the servant of the LORD commanded you, saying, 'The LORD your God is giving you rest and is giving you this land . . . But you shall pass before your brethren armed, all your mighty men of valor, and help them'" (Josh. 1:13–14).

This promise was conditional. God promised to *give* the land to the Israelites but then He instructed them to enter in and to *fight* for it. That is like someone offering to give you a million dollars and then telling you to work the next twenty years in order to obtain it. It doesn't seem like much of a gift!

Perhaps Moses was earlier bewildered by the same paradox:

So I have come down to deliver them out of the hand of the Egyptians, and to bring them up from that land to a good and large land, to a land flowing with milk and honey, to the place of the Canaanites and the Hittites and the Amorites and the Perizzites and the Hivites and the Jebusites. (Exodus 3:8)

So far Moses had not heard anything objectionable. Then the Lord continued: "Come now, therefore, and I will send you to Pharaoh that you may bring My people, the children of Israel, out of Egypt" (Ex. 3:10).

By this point Moses is stammering, "Wait a minute Lord. I thought *you* were going to deliver the children of Israel. Why are you sending *me?*"

God clarified his plan: He was indeed planning to free Israel but He was going to use Moses to do it. Using people to carry out His redemptive work is a practice God uses throughout the Bible and throughout history.

Could God have simply evacuated the cities of Canaan leaving only a welcome mat set outside the city gate? Certainly. God could have sent His death angel to exterminate every living thing in Canaan while the Israelites were still breaking camp east of the Jordan River. God could have put it into the hearts of the Canaanites to pack up their belongings and to move to Mesopotamia before the Israelites arrived. Yet God did not.

God's primary concern was not giving His people land; it was developing a relationship. On Mount Sinai, God said, "You have seen what I did to the Egyptians, and how I bore you on eagles' wings and brought you to Myself" (Ex. 19:4).

The promised land was simply the means God used to establish a unique relationship of trust and obedience with His people. Had the Israelites simply rushed into an evacuated Canaan and moved into the homes and farms, they would have quickly forgotten their Lord. That would have defeated the whole purpose for God delivering them.

Instead, God allowed them to face one challenge after another. At every turn, they realized that without God's intervention, they would fail. Their lives depended on God's presence. The Israelites would therefore do everything possible to ensure God was pleased with them and that He would remain in their midst.

> **The promised land was simply the means God used to establish a unique relationship of trust and obedience with his people.**

God's promises to His people are plentiful. Yet so many Christians do not experience them simply because they don't claim them. Notice some of the profound promises available to every Christian:

- So I say to you, ask, and it will be given to you; seek, and you will find; knock, and it will be opened to you. For everyone who asks receives, and he who seeks finds, and to him who knocks it will be opened. (Luke 11:9–10)

- Come to Me, all you who labor and are heavy laden, and I will give you rest. Take My yoke upon you and learn from Me, for I am gentle and lowly in heart, and you will find rest for your souls. For My yoke is easy and My burden is light. (Matthew 11:28–30)

- Therefore if the Son makes you free, you shall be free indeed. (John 8:36)

- I am the vine, you are the branches. He who abides in Me, and I in him, bears much fruit; for without Me you can do nothing. (John 15:5)

- So Jesus answered and said to them, "Have faith in God. For assuredly, I say to you, whoever says to this mountain, 'Be removed and be cast into the sea,' and does not doubt in his heart, but believes that those things he says will be done, he will have whatever he says. Therefore I say to you, whatever things you ask when you pray, believe that you receive them, and you will have them." (Mark 11:22–24)

These are powerful promises and each is available to every Christian. Yet believers are still reluctant to seek God. They are still soul-weary. They remain in bondage. They are still hesitant to trust God for all the resources He has promised.

No doubt the reason lies in the promises themselves. Quite often God's promises come on the condition of some action on our part. For example: "Draw near to God and He will draw near to you. Cleanse your hands, you sinners; and purify your hearts, you double-minded" (James 4:8).

This is not a blanket promise assuring God's presence regardless of our lifestyles. We are required to cleanse ourselves of our sin and *then* we will experience God's presence. We must be willing to fulfill our obligations to God and not focus exclusively on what we think God's obligation is to us.

Joshua faced this truth at the outset of his leadership. God promised: "Every place that the sole of your foot will tread upon I have given you" (Josh. 1:3). God wasn't going to give Joshua something he did not step out and claim.

The Israelites couldn't remain on the eastern shores of the Jordan River and experience God's promise in Canaan. If they wanted the land, they would have to set foot on it. Joshua learned that God does not grant us His promises by default; we have to claim them.

Our lack of faith is usually the root cause for missing God's promises. As Joshua's life drew to a close, he reminded his people of God's faithfulness: "Behold, this day I am going the way of all the earth. And you know in all your hearts and in all your souls that not one thing has failed of all the good things which the LORD your God spoke concerning you. All have come to pass for you; not one word of them has failed" (Josh. 23:14).

There was no doubt in Joshua's mind that God would always be reliable. The unknown variable was what people would do when God spoke to them. Heavy on Joshua's heart was the hope that his countrymen would stay true to God. He exhorted his nation to uphold their part of the covenant with God:

> And the LORD your God will expel them from before you and drive them out of your sight. So you shall possess their land, as the LORD your God promised you. Therefore be very courageous to keep and to do all that is written in the Book of the Law of Moses, lest you turn aside from it to the right hand or to the left. (Joshua 23:5–6)

All that stood between God's people and God's promises was their obedience. They could choose their fate by trusting God or by doubting Him. The same is true for every believer; God stands ready to fulfill every promise. All He needs to see is our obedience.

FAITH THAT FOSTERS COURAGE

An obvious symptom of weak faith is fear. Fear is the by-product of a lack of trust in God. If fear is rampant anywhere it is on the battlefield. General George Patton said, "Compared to war—all other forms of human endeavor shrink to insignificance."[5]

All that stood between God's people and God's promises was their obedience.

A common characteristic of history's great military commanders has been their personal courage. Great generals have not led from the safety of an obscure command post, miles from the front lines. On the contrary, each demonstrated a courage that inspired his followers.

General Dwight Eisenhower liked to go to the front lines to encourage his soldiers. He said, "It always seems to me that the closer to the front the better the morale and the less the grumbling."

General Patton once came across some officers who appeared more concerned for their own personal safety than they were about leading their men forward. The cantankerous general lambasted them, shouting: "Do you want to give your men the idea that the enemy is dangerous?"[6]

It was said of the Duke of Wellington: "He left the impression that he was perfectly calm during every phase, however serious, of the operation."[7]

British admiral Horatio Nelson observed: "I am of the opinion that the boldest measures are the safest."[8] When Nelson was sent to attack the port at Copenhagen, his commander instructed him that if the fight became too dangerous, he would recall him from action. During the battle, Nelson's lieutenant, Langford, noticed that when the commander's flagship ordered Nelson to withdraw, Nelson ignored it.

Langford persisted in asking Nelson what they should do, to which Nelson responded: "Mr. Langford, I told you to look out on the Danish commodore and let me know when he surrendered; keep your eye fixed on him." But Langford persevered, urging Nelson to heed the supreme commander's signal. Finally Nelson took his lieutenant's telescope and put it to his glass eye. "I really do not see the signal!" he exclaimed. And Nelson fought on to victory.[9]

A biographer of Alexander the Great, conqueror of the known world, noted, "He seems to have been convinced of his invincibility, to have convinced his troops of this and to have imposed this conviction upon the enemy."[10]

One can draw the wrong conclusion about Joshua because God often exhorted His faithful general to "Be strong and of good courage" (Josh. 1:6–7, 9; 10:8; 11:6). Those of us who have never fought in combat may not understand the significance of God's words.

Joshua never demonstrated fear or cowardice. In fact, at times he revealed great courage. But God knows the human heart. No one is immune to fear, especially those in positions of great danger. The fact God spoke such words indicates God knew Joshua needed to hear them. Joshua's greatest fear would be for God to abandon him. Hence God's assurance: "As I was with Moses, so I will be with you. I will not leave you nor forsake you" (Josh. 1:5).

Courage has not been the exclusive domain of military commanders. God's servants have also proven to be heroes in that regard. There is a saying, "The blood of the martyrs became the seed of the church." Throughout history Christians have bravely given their lives rather than yield to fear and compromise their faith.

Preachers such as John Wesley and George Whitefield faced angry mobs of hecklers who threw vegetables, stones, and even dead animals at them while they preached. During a crusade in Chicago, Billy Graham had almost four hundred Satan worshipers enter the stadium with the expressed purpose of rushing the stage and silencing the evangelist.[12] Missionaries such as Jonathan Goforth, Adoniram Judson, and Hudson Taylor buried many of their children on the mission field but refused to be deterred from heeding God's call.

> Throughout history Christians have bravely given their lives rather than yield to fear and compromise their faith.

No one could blame Joshua if he felt intimidated by his enemies. They were purportedly giants!

138

Their cities were fiercely defended. Joshua was not unaware of the dangers of his assignment but, once God spoke, Joshua's confidence was like granite.

The reason some spiritual leaders struggle with fear is because they have not heard their Lord speak. The world is filled with evil people and terrifying situations. If not for God's powerful presence, many Christians would live in constant dread. It is crucial that Christian leaders recognize God's voice. It may be the only thing standing between them and disaster.

Last year Henry was asked to speak in Richmond, Virginia, at a training session for a large group of new missionaries. It was an unusually somber time because of the recent killing of three medical missionaries at the Jibla hospital in Yemen.

As Henry was being driven to the training center to encourage the newly appointed missionaries, the driver's cell phone rang. He pulled off the road and spoke solemnly for several minutes. After his call he turned to Henry, "Henry, we must pray. I just received word that another of our missionaries has been murdered by terrorists in the Philippines."

They did pray, asking God to give them words that would encourage those preparing to go out into a dangerous world for the sake of Christ. God led Henry and his companion, Avery, to share some specific promises from Scripture.

The missionaries responded overwhelmingly with tears of courage and hope. Since those tragic deaths, the mission agency has witnessed a substantial increase in mission volunteers. A word from God in the midst of a crisis makes all the difference!

Fear has an immobilizing effect on Christians, especially on spiritual leaders. What do leaders fear? Failure. Being misunderstood. Humiliation. Responsibility for others' suffering. Criticism.

It was D. L. Moody who cautioned, "We must expect opposition. If you think a great work is to be done here without opposition you will be greatly mistaken."[13] Leaders bear the added pressure of knowing their mistakes can cost others dearly. Leaders have innumerable occasions for fear. They, of all people, must rely on God's wisdom. Their courage must come from God and not from their own self-reliance.

General Ulysses Grant said, "No man ought to win a victory . . . who is not willing to run the risk of defeat."[14] Following God's leading can appear precarious to those who focus on the difficult circumstances before them.

When Joshua began leading his people into Canaan, he remembered how, forty years earlier, his colleagues and the leading experts of his day pronounced the conquering of Canaan too risky and dangerous. Now Joshua was setting out to do exactly that. He was endangering not only his life but the life of every soldier who joined him. If ever he needed courage, now was the time.

FAITH THAT FINDS REST

Just as faith is the remedy for fear, trusting in God also brings a sense of emotional and spiritual rest. Rest was a dominant theme throughout Joshua's life (Josh. 1:13, 15; 11:23; 14:15; 22:4; 23:1).

Joshua spoke to the tribes of Reuben, Gad, and Manasseh about rest:

Remember the word which Moses the servant of the LORD commanded you, saying, "The LORD your God is giving you rest and is giving you this land" (Joshua 1:13).

Later, after the invasion was concluded, we read, "The LORD gave them rest all around, according to all that He had sworn to their fathers. And not a man of all their enemies stood against them; the LORD delivered all their enemies into their hand. Not a word failed of any good thing which the LORD had spoken to the house of Israel. All came to pass" (Josh. 21:44–45).

The concept of rest would have been especially poignant for the Israelites. Their parents had grown up in slavery where exhaustion was a matter of course. The current generation had spent forty years wandering in the wilderness. Their nomadic lifestyle took them everywhere but to the promised land. The tension must have been palpable those four long decades.

Month by month, funeral by funeral, the people gloomily waited for the demise of their unfaithful leaders. Those who had wept with fear at the edge of Canaan now suffered the stares of recrimination from those who were squandering their youth in a barren wilderness.

Then, when the Israelites finally entered Canaan, they experienced anything but rest. Invading enemy territory, they were in a foreign and hostile land. The Israelites had to remain in a state of constant battle readiness. Long marches, grueling days, sleepless nights—the Israelite warriors must have longed for rest.

Physical exhaustion was only one part of the Israelites' weariness. Emotionally, they were stretched to the breaking point. They were separated from their families. They were regularly exposed to violence. They had to kill or be killed. They lost comrades in battle. The possibility of ambush would have kept them constantly on edge.

Spiritually, they were paying a price as well. Oswald Chambers once said, "There is one thing worse than war, and that is sin."[15] While the Israelites were now following God, they were still paying for the sins of their fathers. Instead of enjoying the promised land for the last forty years as God had intended, they were just now struggling to wrest the territory from the Canaanites.

They knew they were not yet where God wanted them to be. The psalmist said, "For forty years I was grieved with that generation, And said, 'It is a people who go astray in their hearts, And they do not know My ways.' So I swore in My wrath, 'They shall not enter My rest'" (Ps. 95:10–11).

And for forty years they did not. The writer of Hebrews, referring to the tragic experience of the Israelites, apprised his own generation of the connection between faith and rest:

> And to whom did He swear that they would not enter His rest, but to those who did not obey? So we see that they could not enter in because of unbelief. Therefore, since a promise remains of entering His rest, let us fear lest any of you seem to have come short of it. For indeed the gospel was preached to us as well as to them; but the word which they heard did not profit them, not being mixed with faith in those who heard it. For we who have believed do enter that rest. (Hebrews 3:18–4:3)

A tormented soul does not experience God's rest. Guilt and anxiety wage war on the spirit, eliminating any hope of peace. Though people surround themselves with safe and comfortable circumstances, they may still lack the restful peace that only God can give. God's rest comes in the midst of all situations. Those who walk closely with God experience a sense of rest that cannot be explained in physical terms.

Hudson Taylor spent much of his missionary life in China facing innumerable hardships. He lived through violent times. He was responsible for the well-being of many missionaries and their families. He had to care for his own family. But, throughout it all, he enjoyed a profound sense of peace and rest.

> **A tormented soul does not experience God's rest.**

He confessed: "The sweetest part, if one may speak of one part being sweeter than another, is the rest which full identification with Christ brings. I am no longer anxious about anything . . ."[16] Such rest comes only by trusting God. God is willing for every person to know this deep, abiding rest that both Joshua and Hudson Taylor experienced.

For nine years, Georgy Slesarev was the lead violinist for the Bolshoi Theater orchestra in Moscow. He was a gifted musician and a committed Christian. Late on the night of January 21, 1935, the secret police arrested him and charged him with crimes against the state. He was accused of actively witnessing to others about his faith in Jesus. His sentence was five years hard labor at the camp at Temir-Tau in Kazakstan, near the Siberian border.

After he had served almost three years, his wife and daughter were allowed to travel to visit him for their one and only time. The day before Slesarev was to see his precious family, the prison warden offered him an incredible opportunity. He could return home with his wife and daughter the next day and assume his old job in the orchestra. The only stipulation was that he promise never to witness of his faith in Christ or associate with Christians again. This he could not do.

He was allowed a brief visit with his wife and daughter the next day, but he could not bring himself to tell them of the offer or of his heart-wrenching refusal. Soon after, he was transferred to a work group doing hard manual labor. His hands that had once played the violin so masterfully were broken and swollen and would never make music again.

In March 1938, Slesarev was convicted of witnessing to fellow inmates about his faith in Jesus. He was sentenced to be executed by firing squad. Shortly before his death, Slesarev confided to a Christian friend in the camp, "My dear brother, don't grieve. Christ has become so close to me. He is closer than He has ever been. My flesh is weak, my body is tired, but this is just a temporary moment in the time of eternity that is soon to open up to me. They have stopped me from playing the violin, but my dear, dear friend, you know, you understand, that they cannot stop the music that plays inside my heart."[17]

The rest God brings to the soul is so deep that nothing, not even a brutal Siberian work camp, can disturb it. The apostle Paul aptly described God's rest as a peace that surrounds your heart and mind and cannot be shaken regardless of your circumstances (Phil. 4:6–7).

It is a peace that comes to those who know they have faithfully carried out God's will. It is experiencing God's pleasure. It is a profound blessing only God can give. Such was the rest Joshua and his people experienced. As they trusted and obeyed God, they entered His rest.

CONCLUSION

Several strong traits defined Joshua, but his most prominent characteristic was his complete trust in God. His faith led him to stand firm for God, even against the jibes and threats of his own colleagues. His faith sustained him even when he could not see the end result of God's promises.

Joshua's faith was not "blind faith" in the sense of being based on what he did *not* know about God. His trust was firmly established by what he *did* understand to be true. Joshua's faith gave him courage to face any enemy. His courage provided compelling testimony to his faith.

Joshua's faith brought the people of God to experience all the promises of God in a land of rest.

Finally, Joshua's faith led him to experience an

indescribable sense of God's rest. God brought peace to Joshua's life. No enemy could rob him of that. Joshua's faith brought the people of God to experience all the promises of God in a land of rest.

FAITH THAT BRINGS WALLS DOWN

- Faith that stands firm
- Faith: One step at a time
- Faith for the future
- Faith that fosters courage
- Faith that finds rest

QUESTIONS FOR CONSIDERATION

1. How would you classify your faith in God—unwavering, strong, fickle, weak, or nonexistent?

2. Is God presently asking you to trust Him for a specific promise? Are you trusting Him one step at a time?

3. What do you sense God wants to do in your future? Does the way you are living your life reflect a confidence God will do what He promised?

4. Is anything currently making you fearful? What does that indicate about your faith in God?

5. Are you presently experiencing God's rest? Why or why not?

EIGHT

INFLUENCE THAT MATTERS

IT WAS THE MOST MOMENTOUS DECISION of the war and no one could make it but him. Five thousand ships were already heading toward their destination. Hundreds of thousands of soldiers were set to advance, awaiting orders from their leader. But weather conditions were dismal. The supreme commander spent a wakeful night listening to the fierce winds howling outside. The rain lashed the side of his trailer in horizontal strips.

Such weather, if unabated, could lead to the loss of thousands of lives. With thousands of vehicles, aircraft, and ships depending on good weather conditions for their mission, there were those who cautiously counseled their leader that postponement was his only recourse. Yet a delay would bring its own problems and possibly more deaths.

As the top leaders gathered the next morning, some urged immediate action. Others advocated caution. Every eye was on the leader knowing his decision would change the course of history. The fate of not only his soldiers, but the destiny of nations hinged on his choice. Finally, he could delay no longer. His generals gathered around him. In a quiet, clear voice he said, "Okay, let's go."

With that a cheer rang out and the men who had been tensely crowded around him moments before burst out the door and raced to their command posts. Thirty seconds after those historic words, the room was empty, except for the man who had uttered them. General Dwight Eisenhower had just ordered the invasion of Normandy. D day had begun and the bloodiest war in human history would soon witness the tide of war shift to the Allies.

A leader's words hold enormous power.

A leader's words hold enormous power. A leader's statement can bind people or it can set them free. A pronouncement from a leader can unite people or it can divide them. A leader's influence can inspire people to accomplish the seemingly impossible or it can demoralize them, rendering them useless. A leader can bless people or curse them.

Joshua's credibility as a leader cannot be overstated. Only a person with tremendous influence could have mobilized a motley crew of nomads to invade a terrifying land teeming with giants and boasting powerful chariots and impregnable fortresses. Influence is a difficult thing to describe.

In the book *Spiritual Leadership: Moving People on to God's Agenda,* we define *influence* as the ability of a leader to move people.[1] Effective leaders take people from where they are and move them to where they ought to be. Secular leaders and spiritual leaders have the same goal of moving people, but they have a completely different agenda.

Secular leaders are motivated by their own objectives or the expectations of their board of governors, their boss, or their colleagues. Economic markets or political factors are significant forces in the secular leadership realm. Conversely, spiritual leaders are driven by God's agenda. Spiritual leaders strive, under God's direction, to move their people to the place God has for them.

Spiritual leaders face two considerable challenges. The first is to clearly identify God's agenda for their people. If they do not understand God's will and if they are unfamiliar with His voice, they will be forced to generate their own vision and hope it pleases God. As we have seen, Joshua regularly communed with God and always understood the Lord's will. His success depended entirely upon this fact.

The second challenge for spiritual leaders comes at the point of influence. Once leaders know where God wants their people to be, how do they move them to get there? We have met numerous leaders who resigned their positions or were relieved of them because they were unable to move their people from where they were to where God wanted them to be.

There are pastors who have left their churches after serving only a few months because the people refused to follow them. To know where your people *ought* to be and yet to be unable to get them there is one of the most frustrating experiences leaders endure.

Joshua knew exactly what God wanted for the Israelites. They were to walk with God in holiness and as they obeyed Him they would capture Canaan. The objective was clear: how to accomplish it was the question. Moses, the revered prophet, was unable to lead these people to fully accomplish God's will.

> To know where your people *ought* to be and yet to be unable to get them there is one of the most frustrating experiences leaders endure.

If the venerable Moses had failed, what hope did Joshua have? If the obstinate people chronically complained and grumbled against Moses, wouldn't Joshua expect to face the same rebellious attitudes from the next generation? Yet Joshua *was* successful. The people *did* follow him. Influence is somewhat of a mystery. Examining Joshua's life will shed some light on how leaders influence followers.

JOSHUA WAS ACCESSIBLE

Winston Churchill once said, "Those who ride in carriages have their own point of view."[2] A leader's accessibility has been the topic of debates for generations. History's leaders have all had to choose what their relationship would be with those they led.

In ancient Rome, General Pompey believed consorting with his men would diminish their esteem for him, so he remained aloof from them. On the other hand, Julius Caesar regularly fraternized with his men and endeared himself to them. When these two antagonists met in an epic clash at Pharsalos, Caesar was victorious even though he had half as many soldiers.

The Duke of Marlborough, though commanding forces of as many as 100,000 soldiers, made every effort to become personally acquainted with them. He would meet with them in groups of 8,000 to 10,000 per day until he had visited all those he was leading into battle.[3]

Despite commanding the largest military force in history, General Eisenhower went to great lengths to make contact with as many of his soldiers as possible. Before D day, he determined that the maximum number of soldiers should see the man who was ordering them into battle. In the months leading up to the massive invasion, Eisenhower visited twenty-six divisions, twenty-four airfields, five naval ships, and numerous hospitals, depots, shops, and other installations.[4]

Before the outbreak of World War Two, Winston Churchill traveled to France to inspect the famous Maginot Line. Churchill had not yet become Britain's prime minister but he was well-known and respected by the French. The French soldiers were bracing themselves for a looming war with Hitler's armies.

Churchill inspected every section of the defensive structure and met with as many of the French troops as he could. His biographer notes: "He knew how to look every man in the eyes as he passed him, thus convincing him he had been recognized by someone already known, even in France, to be a very important person."[5]

Queen Elizabeth I presided over what has been described as a "very visible monarchy."[6] Every year she would go out on a "progress" through various parts of her realm. She would talk with the villagers and actually touch peoples' sores in the hopes of bringing them encouragement and healing.[7] She was greatly esteemed by the British and hers was a highly popular reign.

Many of history's greatest generals have personally led their men in charges against the enemy. Although not always wise from a tactical perspective, by putting their lives at risk and modeling courage in the face of lethal danger, these leaders inspired their men to accomplish magnificent feats.

During the battle of Princeton in the American Revolutionary War, the British routed the Philadelphia militia and appeared to have gained the advantage. Then General George Washington came upon the scene shouting, "Parade with us, brave fellows! . . . There is but a handful of the enemy and we will have them directly."[8] Then the courageous general led his troops in a bayonet charge, riding ahead of them, waving his hat to encourage his men on to victory.

Joshua led his soldiers from amidst their ranks. He did not have a magnificent chariot to ride in or even a powerful stallion to carry him. When he commanded his men to march through the night, he marched with them. When he ordered his men to attack superior forces, he fought with them.

We are never told that Joshua enjoyed a luxurious general's quarters or that his food or his living conditions were superior to his men's. Joshua's men enthusiastically followed him because he fought with them, endured hardships with them, and never asked them to do something he was unwilling to do himself.

JOSHUA REMAINED CONFIDENT

Confidence is a must for an effective leader. People do not follow wishy-washy leaders. Most of history's famous leaders have had confidence in themselves. Some, like George Washington, were endued with robust physical size. Standing six feet four inches tall and weighing over two hundred pounds, it has been said that "his body did not just take up space; it seemed to organize space around it."[9]

John Adams claimed Washington was always asked to lead every national enterprise he was a part of, because he was always the tallest man in the room.[10] It has been said of Dwight Eisenhower that he "looked, acted, and sounded like a president."[11]

> **Confidence is a must for an effective leader.**

However, history books also record a number of accomplished leaders who did not have a large physical stature. Napoleon stood only five feet five inches tall. Queen Victoria was less than five feet tall and complained, "Everybody grows but me."[12] Notice the unimpressive physical description of Ulysses Grant:

> Many of us were not a little surprised to find him a man of slim figure, slightly stooped, five feet eight in height, weighing only 135 pounds. His eyes were dark gray, and were the most expressive of his features. His hair and beard were of chestnut brown color. The beard was worn full, no part

of the face being shaved, but like the hair, was always kept closely and neatly trimmed. His face was not perfectly symmetrical, the left eye being lower than the right. His voice was exceedingly musical, and one the clearest in sound and most distinctive in utterance that I have ever heard. It had a singular power of penetration, and sentences spoken by him in an ordinary tone could be heard at a distance that was surprising. His gait of walking [was] decidedly unmilitary. He never carried his body erect, and having no ear for music or rhythm, he never kept step to the airs played by the bands, no matter how vigorously the bass drums emphasized the accent . . . When not pressed by any matter of importance he was often slow in his movements, but when roused to activity he was quick in every motion, and worked with marvelous rapidity. He was civil to all who came in contact with him, and never attempted to snub anyone, or treat anybody with less consideration on account of his inferiority in rank.

Another observer noted Grant could pass for a "slouchy little subaltern." Yet he "handles those around him so quietly and well, he so evidently has the faculty of disposing of work and managing men, he is cool and quiet, almost stolid and as if stupid, in danger, and in a crisis he is one against whom all around whether few in numbers or a great army as here, would instinctively lean."[13]

Obviously appearances can be deceiving. When he achieved his first command, Grant was so poor he could not afford a proper uniform. He had been considering baking bread for the army to earn a living when he was made a colonel and assigned to Springfield, Illinois, to command the Twenty-first Regiment of volunteers.

This regiment was described as a collection of "vigorous, hardy boys unused to any kind of restraint, every man inclined to think and act for himself."[14] Grant appeared before his men for the first time "'dressed very clumsily, in citizen's clothes—an old coat, worn out at the elbows, and a badly dinged plug hat.' Some of the soldiers began to make fun of him whereupon Grant 'looked at them just for an instant, and in that instant they saw they had a man of nerve to deal with.'"[15]

Despite the slovenly appearance of the new colonel, Grant possessed an inner strength that no one could miss. He never tried to enhance his authority by wearing magnificent uniforms or demanding pomp and ceremony to accompany him. There was just something about him that drew respect from those who knew him.

General Grant also maintained a positive outlook on every crisis he faced, never allowing circumstances to discourage him. The Confederate army battered Grant's forces during an engagement at Shiloh. When a military surgeon commented, "General, things are going decidedly against us," Grant responded: "Not at all, sir, . . . We're whipping them now."[16]

One of his officers asked if he wanted him to prepare their men to retreat and Grant responded: "Retreat? . . . No. I propose to attack at daybreak and whip them."[17] Such confidence inspired his men to anticipate victory as long as their general was leading them. Grant's biographer notes: "Grant had critics aplenty although the troops he commanded were not among them."[18]

The Duke of Wellington stood five feet nine inches tall. While certainly not a giant of a man, his biographer notes, "He had utter confidence in himself and he never lost it."[19] Winston Churchill was said to have "a presence so commanding that he dominated a room the moment he entered it."[20]

Evidently the confidence of great leaders comes not from their size, strength, or social status but from within themselves. Studying these historical figures makes it apparent they gleaned confidence and a positive attitude from a multiplicity of sources.

Some, like Dwight Eisenhower, made a conscious choice to remain steadfastly positive when leading others. Eisenhower said, "I firmly determined that my mannerisms and speech in public would always reflect the cheerful certainty of victory."[21]

Great leaders intentionally maintain optimistic attitudes and a positive demeanor regardless of their circumstances. As a result, they are much more likely to inspire absolute confidence in their troops.

Joshua always spoke boldly of certain victory, but,

> **Great leaders intentionally maintain optimistic attitudes and a positive demeanor regardless of their circumstances.**

unlike most of history's military leaders, the source of Joshua's confidence was not his own military ability—his assurance came from God. His solid faith in God's ability is obvious from his reconnaissance report of Canaan:

> The land we passed through to spy out is an exceedingly good land. If the LORD delights in us, then He will bring us into this land and give it to us, "a land which flows with milk and honey." Only do not rebel against the LORD, nor fear the people of the land, for they are our bread; their protection has departed from them, and the LORD is with us. Do not fear them. (Numbers 14:7–9)

Joshua did not have to force himself to sound confident for the sake of morale; he *was* confident. Throughout the conquest of Canaan, Joshua continually encouraged the people to remain steadfast because God was with them. Just as God's presence ensured Joshua and his soldiers of victory, it simultaneously discouraged and demoralized their enemies (Josh. 2:10–11; 9:24).

People take their cues from their leaders.

People take their cues from their leaders. When leaders grow discouraged and give up, it is totally disheartening for their followers. Leaders often carry more pressure and responsibility than their followers—all the more reason to demonstrate confidence and model a positive attitude. The Israelites took their attitudes from Joshua and because he was so confident in the Lord, they always entered battle assuming they would win.

JOSHUA REMAINED TRUSTWORTHY

Soldiers are accustomed to obeying orders. They generally comply with reasonable instructions. They may even follow questionable commands. But some of Joshua's commands would have seemed downright ludicrous.

Picture a military commander ordering his men to march around an enemy fortress once a day for six days and then circle it seven times on the seventh day. For added measure, Joshua commanded seven priests to blow on rams' horns and the soldiers to shout (Josh. 6:8–21). Such a battle plan would have seemed absurd, except for the knowledge that it came from God.

Imagine a general ordering a soldier and his family to be stoned to death just for keeping some loot from a captured enemy city. It seems excessively harsh, but God had His reasons for commanding it.

Consider a commander in chief ordering his soldiers to march thirty-five kilometers throughout the night so that at sun up they could fight against five kings and their armies, all of whom had enjoyed a good night's sleep (Josh. 10:9).

Visualize a general stopping in the middle of a fierce battle and, in front of his troops and his foes, praying for the sun to stand still so they could complete their victory! (Josh. 10:12–13). These were unusual practices for a general—to say the least! Yet we hear of no complaints from Joshua's men. There was no rebellion or insubordination. They trusted that he knew what he was doing.

Why is it some leaders can call for great sacrifice and exertion and their people seem happy to comply, while other leaders cannot even make minimal requests without stubborn resistance from their subordinates? Usually it is a matter of respect.

Joshua earned his people's trust. He was consistent. He lived among them and fought alongside them. His track record proved he heard from God and that God was blessing his leadership (Josh. 4:14). Joshua's army experienced victory everywhere it went. Joshua had won the trust of his followers. When Joshua was leading, they would follow him anywhere and take on any foe.

GREAT LEADERS EARN LOYALTY

During his final campaign against the French, the Duke of Marlborough was maneuvering against Marshal Villars and his massive French army. Villars was wary of Marlborough, who had defeated the French forces on numerous occasions without ever losing a battle.

The French marshal had carefully stationed himself in a strategic position and confidently awaited Marlborough's advance. Villars was optimistic he would finally inflict a crushing blow on his enemy. Meanwhile Marlborough positioned his soldiers across from the French line in preparation for a frontal assault that everyone agreed would cause Marlborough's army enormous casualties.

It was a somber evening. Soldiers could see their commander was preparing to thrust them into the face of the powerful French army. Every advantage favored the French. The deadly French artillery was positioned to inflict maximum carnage. Yet the soldiers dutifully readied themselves to face almost certain death on the battlefield the next morning.

Many of the soldiers had fought with Marlborough for many years. They had witnessed his brilliant feats. They had met him and heard him speak. They knew he cared for them and that he would not needlessly risk their lives. So strong was their confidence in Marlborough, they unquestioningly complied with his orders, which appeared to be sending them to their deaths.

That night, when darkness fell, a command rang throughout Marlborough's camp: "My lord Duke wishes the infantry to step out!" Soldiers were to hastily prepare for a hard march during the night. Marlborough was not going to hazard a frontal assault after all; his plan was to outflank the French by rapidly marching to the left around the enemy's position.

The infantry ranks were overcome with joy and relief. They quickly realized their commander had pulled a ruse on his opponent. He had never intended to callously forfeit their lives to win a battle. Now their commander needed his men to march post haste in order to seize the strategic advantage. Marlborough's soldiers marched thirty-six miles in sixteen hours and completely outmaneuvered their enemy.[22]

When one reads of such brilliant leadership and of Marlborough's men who would willingly march directly into the murderous cannon fire of their enemies, one is mystified by such a degree of influence. Influential leaders, such as the Duke of Marlborough, did not gain this kind of respect overnight. They earned their influence day by day as they led their people well.

Marlborough was famous for meticulously obtaining the best food and supplies available for his men. The way he treated his troops, coupled with his willingness to face the same hazards they did, won Marlborough the steadfast loyalty and respect of his men. Placed in the context of continuous success, it is no wonder the duke never faced insubordination from those he led.

Modern leaders sometimes misjudge the level of confidence people have in them. Merely occupying a leadership position does not make one a leader. Relying on positional influence is the most anemic way to lead. People may give you the benefit of the doubt initially, but they will be watching to see how and where you are leading them. Almost anyone can obtain a leadership position. But only men and women of integrity and sound character earn the respect that defines a true leader.

> **They earned their influence day by day as they led their people well.**

JOSHUA WORKED WELL WITH ASSOCIATES

It should come as no surprise that Joshua worked well with his associates. God had assigned him to an associate's role for forty years. Moses seemed to struggle in working with other people. He was dismal at delegation and tended to do everything himself (Ex. 18).

Moses faced rebellion from many of his key leaders. The ten "holdout" spies, chief leaders of their respective tribes, did not support him. Interestingly, when these ten men vehemently argued against invading Canaan, Moses did not speak up or interrupt. Even his closest associates, including his siblings Aaron and Miriam, criticized his leadership (Num. 12). Whether it was due to the nature of his followers or the nature of his leadership style, Moses was plagued by insubordination and complaining from all sides during his tenure as a leader.

Joshua seemed better able to deal with associates. Joshua's father-in-law never had to take him aside and teach him how to work with others. It seemed to come instinctively to Joshua. Joshua's associates did not intimidate him though they were strong leaders themselves. We don't read of any adversarial relationships in Joshua's camp. Obviously Joshua knew how to treat associates and how to take them with him as he walked with God.

The refusal to heed advice has been the undoing of many a leader. Queen Victoria's biographer once quipped, "It has always needed courage to inform royalty that some of the people are starving."[23]

One of Joshua's strengths was his willingness to receive counsel from his associates. Joshua sought the assistance of the elders in determining what to do with the Gibeonite messengers (Josh. 9:3–27). Perhaps if Joshua had sought the help of the Lord rather than the elders he would not have been fooled! (Josh. 9:14).

Joshua also worked with the elders of the various tribes along with the high priest to equitably divide the land among the twelve tribes (Josh. 19:51). When Joshua had grown old and was preparing to retire from active leadership, he "called for all Israel, for their elders, for their heads, for their judges, and for their officers" (Josh. 23:2).

> The refusal to heed advice has been the undoing of many a leader.

In an age before loudspeakers and megaphones, it would have been extremely difficult for Joshua to address an entire nation. So he called the leaders together and gave them his final charge. Joshua knew who the influential people of his nation were. He knew how to influence them. He did not alienate them by claiming the credit for their success or by hoarding the limelight. His impact on his associates was so profound that even after his death, they continued to heed what he had said (Judg. 2:7).

Good leaders identify and win over key leaders in their organizations. Carried out with the wrong motive, this can be stark manipulation. But when leaders seek to bring others onside by communicating with them and developing a relationship with them, that is good leadership.

Foolish are the leaders who neglect the influencers of their organizations. It is a mistake to assume everyone will accept a vision merely because it comes from the leader. Joshua was always careful to communicate God's instructions to his leaders, allowing them the opportunity to respond to God and not just to God's messenger.

Admiral Nelson was a master at gaining the respect of his captains. When he assumed command of the British fleet that would fight at Trafalgar, there was unrestrained exuberance among the seventeen thousand sailors upon his arrival.

One of his colleagues said, "Lord Nelson was an admiral, every inch of him . . . yet never was a commander so enthusiastically loved by men of all ranks from the captain of the fleet to the youngest ship-boy."[24]

Within three days of Nelson's arrival, he had dined with every ship captain in his fleet. His chief lieutenants were invited to dine with him any time it was convenient for them to do so. Such attention to his officers and men won him the loyalty of all those who served with him. The result was the greatest naval force of his day.

It can be tempting for leaders to let busy schedules or mounds of paperwork prevent them from spending time with those working under them. Yet this can be a costly oversight. Astute leaders listen carefully to feedback from associates and derive important cues about the organization.

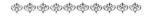

> **Astute leaders listen carefully to feedback from associates and derive important cues about the organization.**

Sagacious leaders schedule regular meeting times with their key people to ensure they are working closely together toward their organizational goals. Joshua was obviously careful to walk with the leaders of Israel, keeping them apprised of what God had said and where they were going next.

JOSHUA INFLUENCED HIS FAMILY

It seems somewhat peculiar that Scripture tells us nothing of Joshua's family. We are told about Moses' parents, his siblings, his wife and children, and even his father-in-law, but we read nothing about Joshua's family. One of the great mysteries of biblical history is why so few children of great leaders followed their parents in serving the Lord. Scripture seems to provide more warnings than positive examples:

- We know Moses had sons, but they never played a prominent role in their nation's history (Ex. 4:20, 24–26).

- Two of Aaron's sons, Nadab and Abihu, were cavalier in serving God and God took their lives in judgment (Lev. 10:1–3).

- The priest Eli had two wayward sons, both of whom died as a result of their sin (1 Sam. 2:12–17; 3:13).

- Samuel's sons were also wicked and could not live up to their father's impeccable reputation (1 Sam. 8:1–5).

History chronicles numerous examples of famous leaders who struggled with their children. President John Adams's oldest son, John Quincy, rescued his parents financially later in life and was also elected president of the United States. But the second son, Charles, spiraled into bankruptcy and alcoholism. His father was so grieved at the life Charles led that he eventually renounced him.[25]

Benjamin Franklin, world-famous inventor and author, became estranged from his son William and would not even attend his wedding nor come to his aid when he was in dire straights.[26]

Winston Churchill suffered a period of painful estrangement from his oldest son Randolph and he actually attempted to prevent the wedding of his daughter Sarah.[27] When Churchill's adult son Randolph had a benign tumor removed, Churchill quipped, "What a pity to remove the one part of Randolph that is not malignant."[28]

> Strangely, many leaders who exert a profound influence on their nation and on the world fail to leave a favorable impression on their own children.

Strangely, many leaders who exert a profound influence on their nation and on the world fail to leave a favorable impression on their own children.

Others, however, were able to lead effectively in their homes as well as on the battlefield. Robert E. Lee Junior remembers the first time he saw his father after he had enlisted as a soldier in the Confederate army:

> The day after the battle of Cold Harbor, during the "Seven Days" fighting around Richmond, was the first time I met my father after I had joined

General Jackson . . . Suddenly I was rudely awakened by a comrade, prodding me with a sponge-staff as I had failed to be aroused by his call, and was told to get up and come out, that some one wished to see me. Half awake, I staggered out, and found myself face to face with General Lee and his staff. Their fresh uniforms, bright equipments and well-groomed horses contrasted so forcibly with the war-torn appearance of our command that I was completely dazed. It took me a moment or two to realize what it all meant, but when I saw my father's loving eyes and smile it became clear to me that he had ridden by to see if I was safe and to ask how I was getting along. I remember well how curiously those with him gazed at me, and I am sure that it must have struck them as very odd that such a dirty, ragged, unkempt youth could have been the son of this grand-looking victorious commander.[29]

It is always an interesting challenge when a child must live up to the reputation of a famous parent. When Dwight Eisenhower was the supreme Allied commander during World War Two, his son John, just graduated from West Point, came to England to visit him.

John, proud of his status as a freshly minted second lieutenant, asked how they should respond to salutes when they both came upon soldiers, as he and his father were of different ranks. "John," Dwight said, "there isn't an officer in this theater who doesn't rank above you and below me."[30]

The Duke of Wellington's son once exclaimed, "Think what it will be like when the Duke of Wellington is announced and only I come in."[31] Some children see God work powerfully in their parents' lives and they are inspired to strive for a similar life themselves. Others, for whatever reasons, grow to resent their parents and choose to take their lives in the opposite direction.

We are not told if Moses' or Joshua's sons became evil or turned from following the Lord. However, it is clear that despite growing up with fathers who were mighty men of God, they did not follow in their steps as prominent leaders themselves.

While there is silence from Scripture about what Joshua's sons did, it is clear what Joshua intended for his family: "And if it seems evil to you to serve the Lord, choose for yourselves this day whom you will serve . . . But as for me and my house, we will serve the Lord" (Josh. 24:15).

Considering Joshua was a man of his word and a man of prayer, and knowing how respected he was, we may assume God blessed his desire for his family.

JOSHUA HAD INFLUENCE WITH GOD

> **It is one thing to have prestige with people; it is quite another to have influence with God.**

It is one thing to have prestige with people; it is quite another to have influence with God. Without question Joshua exerted a tremendous influence upon people, but he also had a rich relationship with God. He was obviously extremely close to the Lord because he regularly and confidently asked for miracles and he routinely received them.

When five Amorite kings united to attack the city of Gibeon, Joshua quickly advanced his army to join the battle. Here was an opportunity for the Israelites to defeat the king of Jerusalem and his allies in one engagement. The fighting was fierce, but God intervened against the Amorites and sent down large hailstones, killing many of them (Josh. 10:11).

The day was beginning to wane and yet the victory was not yet complete. If the enemy were allowed to regroup, they could attack the Israelites at a vulnerable moment in the future. In a most unusual prayer, Joshua asked God to hold the sun still until the battle was complete. Scripture tells us the rest of the story: "And there has been no day like that, before it or after it, that the Lord heeded the voice of a man; for the Lord fought for Israel" (Josh. 10:14).

Herein lies the difference between a secular leader and a spiritual leader. Many of their skills overlap. Both must communicate a sense of vision and direction to their followers. Both must inspire their followers and delegate work to them. Both must lead with confidence.

But only spiritual leaders can draw on God's divine resources for their work. Whether leading secular companies or Christian organizations, spiritual leaders can do so with heaven's resources at their disposal.

During the battle of Oudenarde, the Duke of  Marlborough's army inflicted a crushing defeat on the French forces. Through the brilliant maneuverings of Marlborough and his friend, Prince Eugene, the allied forces encircled almost fifty thousand enemy French soldiers. Such a horrific loss for the French would have inevitably led to an end to the war.

However, just when it seemed the French army would be obliterated, night fell. As Churchill observed: "The mood was valiant, but the hour was late."[32] The Duke's forces tried to completely enclose their enemy but the darkness prevented them from sealing off every exit.

> **Whether leading secular companies or Christian organizations, spiritual leaders can do so with heaven's resources at their disposal.**

At nine o'clock, Marlborough ordered his men to a ceasefire and instructed them to sleep where they were until daybreak. They would await daylight to complete the annihilation. But alas! Morning light revealed that the enemy had escaped, and many of the retreating French soldiers would live to fight another day on more equal terms.

Marlborough ruefully observed: "If it had pleased God that we had had one hour's daylight more at Oudenarde, we had in all likelihood made an end of this war."[33] But even a general as cunning and powerful as Marlborough could not stretch a day, if only by a few minutes!

The Bible identifies certain people who enjoyed an especially intimate walk with God. During the prophet Jeremiah's ministry, God made a revealing statement: "Then the LORD said to me, "Even if Moses and Samuel stood before Me, My mind would not be favorable toward this people" (Jer. 15:1). What an awesome recognition to be viewed by God as one of the great prayer warriors of all time!

Abraham was another such intercessor with God and as a result, God called him His friend (James 2:23). It is one thing for us to take God seriously. It is quite another for God to respond in earnest to us!

In May 1866, Hudson Taylor set sail aboard the ship, Lammermuir, accompanied by his wife and four children and a large contingent of missionaries. They were headed for Inland China. It was to be a four-month voyage to Shanghai. Near the end of their journey, they were struck by a series of violent typhoons. As the storms raged, the ship began breaking apart. The crew became violently seasick. They were demoralized and afraid to venture out on deck to secure the masts and rigging for fear of being washed overboard.

Finally, when the storm did not abate, the captain attempted, by gunpoint, to force the crew back to their posts. Taylor, filled with God's peace, prayed for God to use his life and those of the other missionaries to make a difference in that dangerous situation. He spoke to the captain and crew with a serenity that gave them new confidence and hope. The crew returned to their posts and God miraculously spared the ship, its crew, and all its passengers.

Docking immediately after them was a ship that passed through the same storm and lost sixteen out of a crew of twenty-two.[34] The battered little vessel that limped into port with Taylor and his missionary colleagues bore testimony of a true miracle. Taylor believed God intervened in nature to ensure that the missionaries He had called to China would arrive safely. Certainly they docked in China with a greater trust in God than they had when they first embarked on their journey!

Throughout Taylor's long life, he survived numerous life-threatening crises and diseases. God had a unique assignment for him and God kept him safe regardless of what was happening around him.

Spiritual leaders can exert no greater influence on others than to lead with God's mighty hand upon them. When God chooses to bless leaders' efforts, nothing can stop them. Yet the time people need God most is often when they neglect Him. Hectic schedules and demanding responsibilities drive a wedge between a leader and God. George Müller issued this warning: "A full schedule of preaching, counseling and travel can erode the strength of the mightiest servant of the Lord."[35]

No spiritual leader is exempt from the need to maintain a close relationship with the Lord. Ironically, the busier the leader, the more time should be spent in God's presence.

> **Spiritual leaders can exert no greater influence on others than to lead with God's mighty hand upon them.**

JOSHUA INFLUENCED THE FUTURE

The mark of extraordinary leaders is that their influence outlives them. What they do today determines what happens in the future. Although some people struggle to make a difference in their day, Joshua impacted those living centuries later. Truly this is influence on a grand scale.

> **The mark of extraordinary leaders is that their influence outlives them.**

When Jericho was destroyed, Joshua pronounced a curse on whoever rebuilt the city (Josh. 6:26). The ruins of Jericho symbolized God's judgment on the pagan Canaanites. God had not allowed any survivors from the city except Rahab and her family. Anyone who rebuilt the city would forfeit his sons as a consequence.

Sure enough, many years later in the days of King Ahab, a man named Hiel laid the foundation of Jericho and rebuilt its walls. As he laid the foundation he lost his firstborn son, Abiram. As he hung the doors in the city gates his youngest son, Segub died (1 Kings 16:34). Centuries after Joshua's day, God was still honoring the word He had spoken through Joshua.

Some leaders live with the future in mind. Richard Nixon began taping conversations in the White House because of his paranoia that history would be unkind to him. Ironically, he therefore recorded his own conversations for posterity!

John F. Kennedy was driven by anxiety over how history would remember him. His biographer comments: "History was a goddess Kennedy pursued with notes and short calls to Sorensen or Schlesinger: 'Get that down for the book.' He meant the book he would write after eight years."[36] It was Kennedy's hero Winston Churchill, who, commenting on his own place in history, predicted that history would be kind to him because he intended to write it!

Some people attempt to influence history by their verbosity. They feel compelled to speak to every issue and to reveal everything they know. They assume if they say enough, something they utter will take root and live on in the future. Great leaders do not necessarily talk much, but what they do say is relevant and memorable.

Thomas Jefferson observed Benjamin Franklin and George Washington as the Continental Congress debated and discussed what type of nation they would form. While some politicians spoke often and to every point, Franklin and Washington, arguably the two most respected men in the congress spoke little.

Jefferson said: "I never heard either of them speak for more than ten minutes at a time nor to any but the main point which was to decide the question . . . They laid their shoulders to the great points, knowing that the little ones would follow of themselves."[37]

Great leaders do not necessarily talk much, but what they do say is relevant and memorable.

George Washington may have been a man of few words, but his influence continues over two centuries later. It has been said of him, "More than any great leader in American history before or since, he was accustomed to getting his way and equally accustomed to having history prove him right."[38]

Some leaders blaze into an organization in a fury of dynamic activity but then, like a glowing meteorite, their influence is spent and things return to normality. Such people grasp everyone's attention briefly but later they are forgotten. Others not only impact the people of their generation but their lives and words leave an ongoing legacy.

David Brainerd, a ministerial student, was expelled from Yale College for irreverently criticizing one of his professors. He died of tuberculosis in 1747 at the age of twenty-nine. His life should have merited but a fleeting reference in a footnote of history. But God had led Brainerd to propose to the daughter of the famous minister, Jonathan Edwards.

Edwards was used mightily to help spark the First Great Awakening in the United States through his sermon, "Sinners in the hands of an angry God." Edwards was so taken by his future son-in-law's sanctified life and his passion for evangelizing the native Indians, that when Brainerd died from his exertions, Edwards published his son-in-law's journal. Even now, centuries later, that journal continues to inspire and convict people all over the world.

Leaders are usually people with strong opinions and a willingness to express them. But for spiritual leaders, only the words they speak that come from God will have an eternal impact. All the rest will be merely chaff. Joshua spoke for God. God's words were fulfilled and Joshua's life is remembered.

JOSHUA MOVED PEOPLE TOWARD GOD

Most leaders have a vision for what they would like to see happen among the people they lead. But Joshua used his influence to promote *God's* vision, not his own. As a general in charge of the logistics of an army and concerned with preparing for battle, Joshua would have faced numerous legitimate and pressing concerns. Yet clearly Joshua's first priority was his people's walk with God. He placed this even above his focus on winning the next battle.

On the eve of crossing the Jordan River and entering into Canaan, you might think Joshua would spend every available moment drilling his troops and having them practice with their swords and bows. Instead he declared: "Sanctify yourselves, for tomorrow the LORD will do wonders among you" (Josh. 3:5). Joshua was more concerned about his people's holiness than he was about their battle readiness. Their holiness *was* their battle readiness!

> Joshua was more concerned about his people's holiness than he was about their battle readiness. Their holiness was their battle readiness!

After the Israelites had crossed the Jordan River, you might expect Joshua to act like a wary invader, anticipating a sudden attack by the defending citizens. Instead, he stopped to build a stone monument as a landmark and reminder of what God had done for them at that place (Josh. 4). Then, before going any further with the invasion, Joshua had all the males circumcised as God had commanded (Josh. 5:2–9). It is notable that in the midst of a perilous invasion Joshua should take precious time to meticulously follow God's instructions.

Then Joshua had the people camp at Gilgal, within Canaan, so they could observe the Passover (Josh. 5:10–12). Here they were in the midst of a dangerous invasion; surely they might have put off such religious remembrances until a more opportune time. Yet Joshua made sure they stopped to worship God and to remember all He had done. Obviously he trusted God to protect them. His actions speak volumes about his priorities.

> **His actions speak volumes about his priorities.**

After all the religious observances had been kept, the Israelites did conquer the citizens of Jericho and Ai. But then came another unusual event. After having alerted the Canaanites to their aggressive intentions by destroying two of their cities, you would think Israel would be vigilant in preparation for a counterassault by the hostile allied forces.

But Joshua again stopped to build an altar on Mount Ebal. He gathered the people and "There was not a word of all that Moses had commanded which Joshua did not read before all the assembly of Israel, with the women, the little ones, and the strangers who were living among them" (Josh. 8:35). How unusual! Instead of bracing for a counterattack, they held a worship service along with their women and children!

Obviously Joshua had a different set of priorities from the average general. Joshua ended his term of leadership by urging a gathering of leading citizens to "hold fast to the LORD" (Josh. 23:8). During his entire time as Israel's leader, Joshua's focus was first and foremost spiritual in nature. He was a *spiritual* leader holding the post of a military general.

Throughout Joshua's leadership he was driven by more than the desire to win battles and to be a good administrator. Joshua understood that though he was a layman, not a priest or a prophet, he was still accountable for the spiritual well-being of those placed under his care. He knew that one day he would give an account to the eternal Judge, not for the success of his military maneuvers, but for the spiritual condition of his followers. So, he was diligent to see that they walked closely with God.

We have been privileged to work with many Christian CEOs of major companies who possess this sense of spiritual stewardship. Richard recently spoke on spiritual leadership at the annual convention for Chick-fil-A, whose owner, Truett Cathy, is a devout Christian. Despite the fact he runs a large secular business, he seeks to provide every possible opportunity for his employees to walk with God.

The company pays for its leaders and their spouses to meet in a beautiful location each year to be pampered for several days. During that time Chick-fil-A brings in Christian leaders to preach and teach on relevant subjects. Trained counselors are provided for couples needing marital counseling or individuals looking for encouragement and guidance. No one is forced to agree with or accept Cathy's religious views, but those who desire to walk closely with God have all these resources made available. Truett Cathy is also famous for closing his restaurants every Sunday so that employees can observe the Sabbath. He is an executive whose vocation is secondary to his calling.

CONCLUSION

Leaders are limited in the amount of influence they can exert on their followers. Alexander the Great's soldiers followed him halfway around the world, but they had their limits, and finally refused to follow their general any farther. Joshua was unable to conquer every portion of the Land of Canaan while he led his people, but Joshua was undoubtedly a person of great influence. Nothing stayed the same after Joshua got involved!

Joshua was also a man others took seriously. His enemies certainly feared him. His people followed him. God answered his prayers. God even honored him and his words for the future. When Joshua assumed his leadership role, he oversaw a group of nomads in the desert. When he was finished, he led a nation occupying numerous cities throughout the beautiful land of Canaan.

Everything Joshua did seemed to have a lasting impact. No doubt that was because he stayed on God's agenda throughout his life. God was pleased to honor Joshua because Joshua was eager to honor Him. A life that makes a lasting difference for the kingdom of God—now that's influence!

God was pleased to honor Joshua because Joshua was eager to honor Him.

INFLUENCE THAT MATTERS

- Joshua was accessible.
- Joshua remained confident.
- Joshua remained trustworthy.
- Joshua worked well with associates.
- Joshua influenced his family.
- Joshua had influence with God.
- Joshua influenced the future.
- Joshua moved people toward God.

QUESTIONS FOR CONSIDERATION

1. Are you presently struggling to move your followers forward? If so, why do you think people are not responding more willingly to your leadership?

2. Are you an accessible leader? Would those with whom you work agree with your answer?

3. Do you feel you are a confident and optimistic person? How do you demonstrate these attitudes?

4. Do the people with whom you work trust you? Should they?

5. Are you influencing your family? What positive events or attitudes in your home reflect your leadership?

6. Is there any evidence you have influence with God?

7. How is your life impacting the future?

8. Specifically, how are you helping your coworkers to draw closer to God?

NINE

Joshua's Leadership Principles

HE GREW UP WITH AN INSATIABLE THIRST for fame and glory. His entire life centered on himself and what he planned to achieve. Often he seemed destined to never reach his life's aspiration. As a young man he once was forced to flee for his life when an enemy of his family gained control of the nation and began exterminating his opponents.

At age twenty-six he was captured by pirates and held for ransom. When the cutthroats demanded their price, their arrogant captive boasted he was worth more than twice what they were asking! After his release, he chartered a ship, hunted them down, captured the pirates, and had them all executed. At age thirty-one he looked upon a statue of Alexander the Great and wept at the realization that by the time Alexander was thirty-one, he had already conquered the world. Yet he had accomplished nothing.

He eventually assumed command of an army and set out to conquer expansive new territories. He was a masterful planner of details and meticulously attended to every problem himself. He could dictate four letters simultaneously. Although he never enjoyed robust health, possibly suffering from epilepsy, he showed indefatigable energy in leading his troops.

His biographer describes his relationship with his soldiers: "He did not simply give them orders; he also knew how to convince them . . . he treated them as comrades. They felt he knew them and that they could rely on him."[1] His men eagerly followed him. He exhibited cheerfulness, strength and confidence that inspired his soldiers and drew them to him like a magnet.

When his men began faltering in the face of their enemies, he encouraged them and filled them with new resolve. When facing a formidable enemy, he would charge to the front of the most perilous action, hollering the names of his officers, encouraging them to take heart and to follow his lead. He was generous with rewards and promotions. Though his schemes were not always successful, "his plans were seldom totally frustrated."[2]

His victorious track record inspired awe, both in those he led and in those he fought. He conquered the territory of modern France, capturing eight hundred towns and defeating three million armed men in the process.[3] He seized land in what is now England, as well as North Africa and Asia. In his most pivotal battle, he faced an army of forty-seven thousand men with only twenty-two thousand soldiers, and won a decisive victory through a daring strategy.[4] His success was so remarkable a statue was erected in his honor entitled, "To the undefeated god."[5]

But the more exalted he became the more he grew to disdain those who groveled before him. He accepted his people's flattery and praise as a matter of course. He grew to believe he was so superior to others that he needed no one. In a spirit of detached arrogance, he dismissed his bodyguard. This fateful step led to his brutal assassination by twenty-three Roman senators.

Julius Caesar had conquered all his enemies but the same traits that made him successful also led to his demise. His biographer notes, in what would seem to be an understatement, that Caesar developed an "immense self-sufficiency."[6] Despite his oratorical genius, his military prowess, and his masterful leadership skills, he reached the limit of what even a brilliant man could do. His illustrious life came to an abrupt and brutal end at the hands of his alleged friends and colleagues.

Joshua practiced many of the leadership skills that are highly praised in military and corporate circles today.

There is no doubt God was the reason for Joshua's magnificent success. Without divine guidance and intervention, Joshua and his ragtag band of ill-equipped soldiers would have been dashed to pieces at the hands of the Canaanites. Joshua never took credit for his military success and we would be remiss in granting it to him now. But God did develop Joshua into an outstanding leader. Joshua practiced many of the leadership skills that are highly praised in military and corporate circles today.

At times Christian leaders tend to "spiritualize" God's work by saying, "It is all God and nothing to do with me!" It is true that everything they do of eternal significance has been inspired, empowered, and enabled by God, but this attitude can simply be an anemic excuse for poor leadership. Pastors and Christian business leaders can excuse a halfhearted effort for their organization by "waiting on God to do what only He can do."

Some Christian leaders never strive to improve their leadership skills lest it appear they are relying too heavily on their own strength. Such an attitude ignores God's command to do *everything* as though we are doing it for Him (Col. 3:23).

God is sovereign. He can and will work through any person He chooses. Those who assume God will use them for His service regardless of their skills, education, or effort may be as disappointed as the indolent student who didn't bother to study for her exam and instead, "trusted in the Lord!" Leaders shortchange themselves and their followers when they grow complacent and neglect to improve their leadership abilities.

> **Leaders shortchange themselves and their followers when they grow complacent and neglect to improve their leadership abilities.**

We have known pastors who have loved God and loved their congregations, but were poor leaders. They were disorganized, wasted time, did not plan ahead, and they were careless in keeping appointments. They were weak at delegation; their sermons were disjointed and poorly delivered. Not surprisingly, their congregations were small and spiritually undernourished.

Often their people stoically suffered through mismanaged church programming because they loved their pastor, but they needed him to be so much more. Please hear us: not all small churches are the result of poor leadership, but today's generation is desperate for spiritual leadership and people will go where they find it. Using the same principle, being a Christian businessman does not guarantee God's blessing on your business if you overlook solid business practices. Leadership skills are important in the kingdom of God!

Joshua's life was a good combination of wise leadership and God's blessing. Joshua obviously enjoyed God's favor, but he also allowed God to work on his character. God did not choose to work through Joshua "just as he was." Rather, He chose to work *in* Joshua as He worked *through* him.

> **Joshua's life is a good combination of wise leadership and God's blessing.**

God took an uneducated, inexperienced slave from Egypt, and walked with him through the years. As a result, Joshua emerged as an extremely effective spiritual leader. Joshua's life demonstrated tremendous leadership skills. We could greatly benefit from studying the work God did in Joshua. This chapter will focus on the leadership skills God built into his life.

JOSHUA GREW DURING TRANSITIONS

Life is in constant flux—the pace slackens, then quickens. Successful leaders master times of transition. History's military heroes were not constantly at war. They also had to deal with peacetime (though some spent as little time at this as possible!).

The Duke of Marlborough could not be defeated in open conflict on the battlefield, but he could be brought low by the insidious intrigues in parliamentary back rooms. General George Patton confessed, "In peace I am useless."[7] General Ulysses Grant was an effective leader in battle, but "as soon as wealth came his way—good sense deserted him."[8]

Joshua spent a great deal of his life in transition. He was a slave until Moses arrived in Egypt to deliver the Israelites from Egyptian bondage. Then he spent the next forty years preparing for the next phase of God's plan. During that time, only two adults made the transition into the promised land. Everyone else perished. How did Joshua (and Caleb) survive the dramatic changes taking place when everyone else was losing heart and dying? Joshua did two things.

1. JOSHUA KEPT HIS EYES ON GOD

Joshua kept his eyes on God regardless of the shifting circumstances around him. He knew that although the heavens and earth might change, God would remain constant (Mal. 3:6). Times change. Governments change. Trends and economies change. People change. Placing one's hope and trust in any of these things is foolish.

Joshua knew better; he understood God's sovereignty over his life while he dwelt in Egypt. God was Lord of his life in the wilderness and He would still reign over the universe when Joshua entered Canaan. That would never change.

2. JOSHUA MADE THE MOST OF GROWTH OPPORTUNITIES

Joshua made the most of his growth opportunities. He did not sit and stagnate waiting for something big to happen. Even during the long transition period in the wilderness, he followed God diligently and nurtured God's presence in his life (Num. 27:18). Times of tranquil solitude, rare as they are, provide tremendous opportunities to grow closer to God. During Israel's wanderings, others were simply putting in time. But Joshua was growing, and when the transition time ended, he was the most prepared person in the entire nation to serve as leader.

Transition times should never be squandered. God may use such times to bring about tremendous growth. Take advantage of unexpected "forced downtime." If an injury pulls you out of your workplace, as you recuperate seize the opportunity to read books that will develop your skills and knowledge. If your church is "between pastors," there are still numerous ways to reach out and minister to your community during the interim period. Wise leaders maximize transition periods by continually growing and seeking the Lord, so they are fully prepared for what comes next.

> **Wise leaders maximize transition periods by continually growing and seeking the Lord, so they are fully prepared for what comes next.**

JOSHUA BUILT ON THE PAST

Throughout history, people in leadership positions have often been more concerned with protecting what already existed than pursuing something new. Sir Francis Bacon observed of Queen Elizabeth I, "Her Majesty loveth peace. Next, she loveth not change."[9] Her royal secretary, Robert Beale, warned his successor to "avoid being new-fangled and a bringer-in of new customs."[10] Not surprisingly one of her mottos was *Semper Eadem*—"always the same."[11]

It was said of Queen Victoria: "She hated any change even when it was for the better."[12] While there may have been times in history when successful leaders could be slow to embrace progress, in today's rapidly changing environment, a leader resistant to change is an albatross rather than an asset.

GOOD LEADERS USE THE PAST AS A RESOURCE

It is also true that good leaders don't try to reinvent the wheel. Much of today's leadership literature implies that the mark of a good leader is an automatic dissatisfaction with the status quo. A commonly held maxim is that leaders constantly seek change and relish transforming their organizations. Many pastors cite Isaiah 43:18–19: "Do not remember the former things, nor consider the things of old. Behold, I will do a new thing."

This type of leader believes that upon arriving at his new organization he must radically transform everything. The problem with this mindset is that the result is a waste of the accumulated efforts made in the past. Rejecting an organization's history can reflect a callous disregard for what God has already accomplished.

Organizations often mistakenly assume when replacing a leader that they must enlist someone completely opposite to his or her predecessor. If the former CEO was a "people person," the next one must be a "systems person." If the previous pastor was keen on discipleship, the next pastor must be passionate about evangelism. Although there is sometimes a need to shore up deficiencies in current or former leaders, it can be a devastating mistake to reinvent your organization every time you obtain a new leader.

Any organization under God's guidance will be following a plan God has initiated. He may add people with new skills to strengthen His work, but He is unlikely to keep changing the plan. Consider the following scenario we have seen played out in many churches:

> The original pastor is a highly personable man—he knows everyone and is dearly loved by his congregation. Although he is somewhat disorganized, the church grows and hires additional staff. When the much-loved cleric retires, a pastor search committee is formed and is immediately inundated with the seemingly prudent advice: "You need a pastor who will be strong in areas in which your last pastor was weak." So they focus on prospective pastors with strong administrative skills and backgrounds in management and finance. They find such a person and then eagerly commission him to "clean up the mess" from the former minister.
>
> Sure enough, the new pastor is determined to straighten up the hitherto loose administrative practices. He fires a few staff members and replaces them with more "effective" personnel. He introduces stricter accountability on staff and church committees. Longtime volunteers are replaced with paid staff for the sake of efficiency. The pastor spends much more time in the office than his predecessor, though he is rarely sighted at the hospital or seniors' home. While the church is unquestionably run more proficiently than it was before, members begin grumbling that things don't "feel like they used to." Some longtime members think about joining a smaller church where they won't "feel like a number."

What happened? God built a church around a ministry of personal caring and close relationships. The people who joined the church did so because they *liked* that kind of ministry. Over the years, the church attracted people who appreciated and responded positively to that leadership style. The newer believers had been drawn to Christ by the love and warmth of the congregation. When the church hired its new minister, it suddenly had a leader who did not match the people he had been enlisted to lead. This is a phenomenon we've seen many times, not just in churches but also in schools and businesses.

❀❀❀❀❀❀❀❀❀❀

Today's organizations must address their weaknesses while honoring the strengths and values they have gained over the years.

❀❀❀❀❀❀❀❀❀❀

We are not suggesting organizations should never change or that each succeeding leader should be a clone of his predecessor. Obviously each new leader brings unique talents and skills and this is crucial. Organizations need to grow and mature and that calls for different styles of leadership. But over time, organizations take on values that become deeply ingrained in their fabric. Those values are ignored at the leader's peril!

Today's organizations must address their weaknesses while honoring the strengths and values they have gained over the years. New leaders must be cautious lest they trample on the values God has instilled in an organization. The most successful leaders of tomorrow will be those who master today's transitions.

Joshua Remained True to God's Plan

Joshua did not charge in with a whole new agenda for Israel. He remained true to God's original plan for His people. Scripture repeatedly says Joshua "left nothing undone of all that the LORD had commanded Moses" (Josh. 11:15). "There was not a word of all that Moses had commanded which Joshua did not read before all the assembly of Israel" (Josh. 8:35).

Joshua knew God had spoken to Moses; he had witnessed it personally! He understood his role to be a part of God's ultimate plan. Joshua was not *the* plan. Understanding this truth would help so many people to find God's will. People should not ask: "What is God's will for my life?" but "What is God's will and how should I adjust my life to it?"

This was Joshua's mind-set. When Joshua finally conquered Canaan and divided the land among the tribes, he clearly understood this to be a fulfillment of God's word to his ancestors many years earlier. Joshua was a much different leader than Moses had been. Joshua accomplished things Moses never did. He led the people to places Moses was unable to take them. There was much that was new under Joshua's leadership. However, Joshua applied his unique, God-given skills to the plan God had initiated long before he was born.

Great leaders don't disparage what has been handed to them by previous generations; they build on it. Alexander the Great took the army his father, Phillip, had meticulously trained and organized, and with it he conquered the world.

Abraham Lincoln sought to unite a deeply divided nation. At Gettysburg the beleaguered president began one of history's greatest speeches: "Four score and seven years ago our fathers . . ." He went on to link current events to his nation's beginning, to the beliefs and decisions of the founding fathers. Wisely connecting his present efforts to the past, Lincoln was dramatically impacting the future.

Great leaders don't disparage what has been handed to them by previous generations; they build on it.

JOSHUA WAS A TEACHER

Good leaders are also good teachers. Part of Joshua's influence came from the way he instructed his people. He never assumed they would automatically know what to do or why they should do it. As soon as Joshua was installed as Israel's new leader, he began reminding his people what God had been saying to them (Josh. 1:13).

After they conquered the city of Ai, Joshua gathered the people on Mount Gerizim and Mount Ebal. Then Joshua personally read all of God's law to the people (Josh. 8:34). "There was not a word of all that Moses had commanded which Joshua did not read before all the assembly of Israel, with the women, the little ones, and the strangers who were living among them" (Josh. 8:35).

The practice of continually reminding the people of God's promises and commandments characterized Joshua's entire ministry. Even at the end of his life Joshua meticulously exhorted the people to obey God (Josh. 23:1–24:28).

It has been said that Napoleon's defeat at Waterloo was due largely to the fact he never taught his generals to lead as he did. On the other hand, his

Good leaders are also good teachers.

nemesis Horatio Nelson constantly encouraged and trained those who served under him. An observer once commented on how the skilled captain educated the inexperienced and nervous young boys in his crew:

> The timid he never rebuked . . . but always wished to show them he desired nothing of them that he would not instantly do himself: and I have known him say—"Well sir, I am going a race to the mast-head and beg I may meet you there." No denial could be given to such a wish and the poor fellow instantly began his march. The captain never remarked on the manner in which the mast was climbed and, meeting the boy at the top, began instantly speaking in the most cheerful manner and saying how much a person was to be pitied who could fancy there was any danger, or even anything disagreeable, in the attempt. After this excellent example, I have seen the timid youth lead another and rehearse his captain's words.[13]

Nelson regularly took time to instruct his young recruits not only in seamanship but also in other matters such as proper hygiene so they would avoid illness. When invited to dine with the local governor or other dignitaries, he would always bring one of his young sailors with him. He would explain to his exalted host: "Your Excellency must excuse me for bringing one of my midshipmen, as I make it a rule to introduce them to all the good company I can as they have few to look up to, beside myself, during the time they are at sea."[14] Is it a coincidence that Nelson eventually developed a fleet that was invincible?

The apostle Paul made the ability to teach a requirement for anyone serving as an overseer in the church (1 Tim. 3:2). Leaders who are too busy or impatient with their people tend to bark out commands and become agitated when performance levels don't meet their standards. Often these leaders end up doing the job themselves—to make certain it is "done right." They neglect all kinds of opportunities to teach the skills they find lacking.

It is not enough to suggest a seminar or a relevant book. Some skills are best learned on the job. Often the best teacher on the job site is the person in charge. An investment of time teaching someone today can pay huge dividends tomorrow.

COMPETITION OR COOPERATION?

Some leaders refuse to invest in training their staffs for fear people will become overqualified for their jobs, demand more money, or be snatched up by the competition. However, true spiritual leaders understand their stewardship of each life God places under their influence. Spiritual leaders have a mandate to help their people become all God intends for them to be (Ezek. 34:1–10).

Inevitably other organizations will recognize quality employees and seek to hire them. However, if no other organization is impressed with your staff enough to want to hire them, that may be an indictment of either your hiring or your training practices! It ought to be a matter of great satisfaction for you to lead men and women who are highly coveted by other organizations. One of the greatest rewards of your leadership career may be that you help develop some of the top leaders in your field, who influence organizations all across the country and around the world.

We know college and seminary presidents who regularly see their vice presidents called as presidents to other schools. Some of our pastor friends can count dozens of former associates who now serve as senior pastors elsewhere. In the big scheme of things—God's kingdom—this is influence at its best. God's work is not about competition—it's about cooperation for the sake of a higher calling.

> **Spiritual leaders have a mandate to help their people become all God intends for them to be.**

JOSHUA USED LEADERSHIP TOOLS

Stories and symbols have enormous value as leadership tools. A well-told story can communicate far more than a two-hundred-page policy manual. Stories capture people's imaginations. People remember stories years after hearing them, though they may not remember the instructions they were given five minutes earlier. Stories are symbols. They can represent what is valuable to an organization. Good leaders learn how to incorporate stories into their leadership style.

JOSHUA TOLD STORIES

Joshua regularly told the tale of how God rescued the people of Israel from Egypt and how He brought them into the promised land. Some of the veteran soldiers must have grinned and nodded their heads knowingly as their revered general began telling the familiar epic once again.

Some of his longtime followers could probably recite portions of the tale with their leader. There may have been certain points in the narrative—for example, when the ten spies frightened the people from trusting God—that the old soldiers grew emotional as Joshua recalled those painful moments.

The story was important, because it explained how the people had come to be where they were. There were various ways Joshua could have explained how God had walked with them, but Joshua wasn't a trained orator, a writer, or even a priest. He didn't present the data of their lengthy pilgrimage on a flip chart or from a dusty book. He was a layman who walked with God, so he simply chose to tell the story.

JOSHUA USED PHYSICAL SYMBOLS

The use of other symbols is also important. A symbol is a powerful tool in the hands of a seasoned leader, whether it is a story, an actual physical monument, or a symbolic action. Joshua was a master at using symbolism to drive home truths to his followers.

When the Israelites miraculously crossed the Jordan River into Canaan, Joshua instructed a man from each tribe to collect a stone from the riverbed. Those stones were carried on the men's shoulders until they reached Gilgal, where Joshua built a monument. Joshua said:

> This may be a sign among you when your children ask in time to come, saying, "What do these stones mean to you?" Then you shall answer them that the waters of the Jordan were cut off before the ark of the covenant of

the LORD; when it crossed over the Jordan, the waters of the Jordan were cut off. And these stones shall be for a memorial to the children of Israel forever. (Joshua 4:6–7)

Though they had just experienced a stupendous miracle, Joshua knew the following generations would not appreciate what had happened unless it was explained to them. Whenever young Israelites came upon the crude monument, it was an opportunity for their parents to retell their awesome experience of crossing the Jordan River. Many generations later, that weathered stone monument would still stand as a testimony to God's miraculous work.

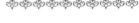

A symbol is a powerful tool in the hands of a seasoned leader.

At the close of his leadership term, Joshua again used a stone as a symbol. He gathered the people and exhorted them to serve the Lord and to "put away the foreign gods that are among you, and incline your heart to the LORD God of Israel" (Josh. 24:23). Then he made a solemn covenant with the people as they swore their allegiance to God.

Once they had fully committed themselves to following God, Joshua set up a large rock under an oak tree near the tabernacle. He called the stone a silent witness to the commitment they had solemnly made with God. Every time they saw the stone in the future it would be a reminder of their sacred vow (Josh. 24:27).

In a different tone, Joshua decreed that the city of Jericho was never to be rebuilt (Josh. 6:26). The once formidable city was to lie in perpetual ruin as a stark reminder of God's judgment. No one could pass by that once mighty city without the chilling recollection of God's awesome power.

After Joshua's time, when the children of Israel ignored Joshua's plea and turned away from God, God allowed their enemies to torment and defeat them. Even as the Israelites were fleeing in fear from their enemies, the ruins of Jericho stood as a somber testimony of what God could do for His people when they walked faithfully with Him.

Likewise, when the Israelites executed the king of Ai as well as the king of Jerusalem and his four royal allies, Joshua commanded that a large mound of stones cover their graves (Josh. 8:29, 10:27). These mounds gave silent testimony to the perils of waging war against God and His people. After Israel's conquest of Canaan, the promised land was littered with graphic reminders of God's judgment on his foes.

JOSHUA USED SYMBOLIC ACTIONS

Joshua also used symbolic actions to great effect. During the early stages of the Israelite invasion, Jerusalem's king gathered four fellow kings and united their armies to resist Joshua's forces. This was a powerful army led by five monarchs, yet with God's intervention Joshua's forces defeated them.

In the aftermath of the enemy rout, the five kings hid in a cave at Makkedah until the Israelites discovered them (Josh. 10:16). After the battle, Joshua presented the five kings to his people. The Israelites had once been terrified of these men and their armies and that fear had cost them forty years in the wilderness.

To emphasize that there was no reason to fear God's enemies, Joshua had the five kings lay on the ground. Then Joshua had the captains of his army put their feet on the kings' necks, graphically symbolizing the total submission of these rulers to the Israelites (Josh. 10:24). It was humiliating for these once proud sovereigns but it was an unbelievable triumph for Joshua's forces.

Clearly *no one* and *nothing* could withstand them when God was fighting for them. Joshua then killed the kings and hung their bodies from trees until evening so the entire army could witness the total subjugation of their once proud enemies. Although the military practices of that day are barbaric to us today, the enormous positive effect of such symbolism is obvious.

The young Israelite soldiers had grown up in abject fear of these kings. They had spent year after year squandering their youth in a barren desert while their aging parents feebly justified their disobedience to God by explaining that Canaan was populated with fierce, undefeatable giants. But now they had seen these "giants" up close. Even their kings were ordinary men who could be humbled by God. Joshua wanted to remove any question from his soldiers' minds that when they walked obediently with God they were invincible. Throughout the remainder of Joshua's leadership there is no mention of his soldiers ever fearing their enemies.

GREAT LEADERS SEIZE SYMBOLIC MOMENTS

Throughout history, great leaders have known how to seize symbolic moments. At the close of the Revolutionary War, George Washington heard of a secret meeting being called by dissatisfied officers. Congress, struggling with finances, had not yet been able to keep some of its promises to its soldiers.

Washington arrived unexpectedly at the large military barracks at New Windsor on March 12, 1783. He marched directly up to the lectern and read them a speech imploring them not to do anything foolish but to trust in the good will of the Congress. He concluded by saying: "You will, by the dignity of your conduct, afford occasion for posterity to say, when speaking of the glorious example you have exhibited to mankind, 'Had this day been wanting, the world had never seen the last stage of perfection to which human nature is capable of attaining.'"[15]

Then Washington pulled out a letter and with a final flourish, laden with drama, slowly put on his new eyeglasses. Looking steadily at his men he said: "Gentlemen, you must pardon me, I have grown gray in your service and now I find myself going blind."[16]

As he solemnly left the building, the poignancy of the moment was lost on no one. Here was the greatest man of their age. He had willingly given his youth for the American cause. It seemed unimaginable for them to continue advocating their own grievances. Washington could have recounted all his sacrifices and how he, too, had justifiable concerns. But this one, simple act said it all. Leaders become masters of communication by capturing such symbolic moments.

A variety of symbols can be used to undergird a message. A leader can flog equality all she wants but removing the "Reserved for President" sign from the front of her parking space will communicate the message far more effectively. Asking everyone to

> **Throughout history, great leaders have known how to seize symbolic moments.**

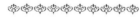

183

pitch in to help is great, but when the CEO stoops and picks up garbage out-side the front door, the gesture speaks volumes. Announcing you have an "open door policy" is one thing; actually keeping your door open symbolizes the reality. Anyone can say they care about their employees, but taking the time to walk about the factory or office complex and chat with them indi-vidually proves the point. Specific actions leaders take will communicate their priorities far more clearly than an impersonal memo.

JOSHUA REMAINED FOCUSED

From the moment Joshua took the reigns of leadership no one had any ques-tion about his intentions. Joshua clearly understood God's assignment: pre-pare God's people to conquer the land of Canaan and then occupy it as a holy nation for God's glory. The Israelite general never lost sight of the goal God set before him. There were no distractions. There were no delays. There were no excuses. Regardless of how formidable the enemy appeared, Joshua relentlessly moved forward to accomplish his goal. Joshua led his people onward with dogged persistence, much like General William Tecumseh Sherman who once gave the command for "every man to look as numerous as possible."[17]

During the Civil War, the Union generals seemed uncertain of their war aim. Despite their superiority in manpower and supplies, the top command-ers were reluctant to attack their enemy. Union generals seemed preoccu-pied with avoiding defeat by General Lee, protecting the capital, slowly wearing away Southern resolve, or capturing strategic positions through tac-tical maneuvering. That changed after President Lincoln appointed Ulysses S. Grant as the supreme commander of the Union army.

Grant knew his task was singular: to destroy the Confederate army. General Sherman said of Grant, "He fixes in his mind what is the true objective and abandons all minor ones."[18] His biographer noted: "He saw his goals clearly and moved toward them relentlessly."[19] Grant's instruction to his associate General Meade was pointed: "Wherever Lee goes, there you will go also."

After Grant's appointment, when several Confederate officers disparaged Grant's validity as a serious threat, Confederate General Longstreet cautioned them:

> Do you know Grant? . . . Well I do. I was with him for three years at West Point, I was present at his wedding, I served in the same army with him in Mexico, I have observed his methods of warfare in the West, and I believe I know him through and through. And I tell you we cannot afford to underrate him and the army he now commands. We must make up our minds to get into line of battle and stay there, for that man will fight us every day and every hour till the end of this war.[20]

Grant knew his goal and he pursued it rigorously. While some decried the number of casualties Grant seemed willing to sustain, no one could deny his unwavering dedication to accomplish his mission.

EFFECTIVE LEADERS FOCUS ON THEIR PURPOSE

Effective leaders know the purpose of their organization and they focus on pursuing it. Leaders can be easily distracted by secondary matters and inadvertently neglect to accomplish their primary task. It can be tempting to concentrate so intently on the means to the end that you forget what the end is!

Preparing to attain a goal or declaring one's intent to reach a goal is not the same thing as achieving it. Some leaders focus so much attention on building teamwork in their organization that they indeed end up with a team, but it's a team that fails to accomplish its mission.

Some leaders concentrate on problem solving to the extent that they lose sight of their goal. Some are good at planning; others are good at doing. We are not advocating a single-minded approach that excludes the important matters of team building and problem solving. However, effective leaders know that many important activities will engage their attention, but all are secondary to the primary objective of accomplishing the organization's purpose.

185

Leaders can be easily distracted by secondary matters and inadvertently neglect to accomplish their primary task.

We know many well-meaning CEOs and pastors who have been fired. In some cases those dismissing them were their friends. The fundamental issue was not how hard they had worked or whether they had integrity. The problem was that they were not getting the job done. There are many things to admire about Joshua and his leadership style, but one thing stands out: he stayed focused on his God-given mission.

JOSHUA HAD PASSION

Joshua was a passionate leader. He believed deeply in what God had called him to do. Today we frequently use dichotomies to categorize people: "He's a feeler" or "She's a thinker"; "He's task oriented" or "She's people oriented." Great leaders have emerged from each of these categories. From what we know of Joshua, he may well have been a "feeler." He certainly cared deeply about fulfilling God's assignment. The apostle Peter was a feeler; the apostle Paul was a thinker. Both were extremely passionate men. Leaders don't have to be feelers to be passionate about what they do.

JOSHUA WAS NEVER COMPLACENT

Throughout Joshua's leadership career we catch glimpses of his passion. We see Joshua's passion when he confronted the heavenly visitor who was brandishing a sword. Without hesitation and with no contingent of soldiers backing him up, Joshua approached the messenger and demanded to know, "Are you for us or for our adversaries?" (Josh. 5:13).

When the ten spies returned from Canaan and began to terrify the Israelites with their accounts of giants, Scripture says, "But Joshua the son of Nun and Caleb the son of Jephunneh . . . tore their clothes; and they spoke to all the congregation of the children of Israel, saying . . ." (Num. 14:6–7). That's passion! Joshua and Caleb knew what was at stake. This was a pivotal moment. Tearing one's clothes symbolized great grief and sorrow over what was being done. If the Israelites failed to trust God now, the consequences would be severe.

When the Lord withdrew His presence from Joshua's army during their attack on the city of Ai, Joshua's forces were defeated. In a feverish outburst, Joshua again tore his clothes (he must have kept a seamstress on retainer), put dust on his head, and fell to the ground. He implored God:

> Alas, Lord GOD, why have You brought this people over the Jordan at all—to deliver us into the hand of the Amorites, to destroy us? Oh, that we had been content, and dwelt on the other side of the Jordan! O Lord, what shall I say when Israel turns its back before its enemies? For the Canaanites and all the inhabitants of the land will hear it, and surround us, and cut off our name from the earth. Then what will You do for Your great name? (Joshua 7:7–9)

Joshua was passionate in failure as well as in success. He was never complacent with either.

Another sign of Joshua's passion for his work was his habit of rising early to perform his most difficult tasks. Whether it was attempting to cross the Jordan River, re-attacking the city of Ai, or looking to uncover a traitor in his ranks, Joshua rose early to start his day (Josh. 6:12, 7:16, 8:10). One mark of passionate leaders is the way they begin the day. Those who awaken in anticipation of what God

Joshua was passionate in failure as well as in success. He was never complacent with either.

might do, still have their passion. Those who reluctantly or grumpily begin the day may no longer expect God to intervene in their lives. To them it is "just another day."

Joshua remained passionate to the end of his life. At the close of his tenure he left Israel with this entreaty: "And if it seems evil to you to serve the LORD, choose for yourselves this day whom you will serve . . . But as for me and my house, we will serve the LORD" (Josh. 24:15). The passion for knowing God and doing His will never subsided within Joshua.

WHY IS PASSION IMPORTANT?

People who accomplish great things are those who care a great deal about what they are doing. An apathetic leader is a contradiction in terms. Whether pastors, CEOs, or school principals, the people we meet who are making a difference in their worlds are passionate about their work.

Conversely, we meet pastors who tell us their churches are not growing and nothing good seems to be happening. Their monotone, impassionate demeanor hints that the stagnant conditions may originate in these pastors' attitudes.

PASSION CAN BE TENDER

Spiritual leaders are often those whose hearts are so tender they are never far from laughter or from tears. D. L. Moody was a giant of a man but a leader with an extremely sensitive heart. "It is true, as his daughter-in-law discovered, that if he asked for 'Rock of Ages' and she played 'Yankee-Doodle' slowly and sorrowfully, he would wipe tears from his eyes."[21] Of course this may also indicate that great leaders are not always great musicologists. Ulysses Grant used to say that he only knew two songs: "One was Yankee Doodle and the other one wasn't."[22]

After the Battle of Waterloo, the Duke of Wellington had the officers' table set for dinner and then anxiously looked up each time the door opened to see if it was one of his friends returning from battle. When the chief physician, Dr. John Hume, finally arrived to give the preliminary casualty report, the doctor remembered:

> As I entered, he sat up, his face covered with the dust and sweat of the previous day, and extended his hand to me, which I took and held in mine, whilst I told him of Gordon's death, and of such of the casualties as had come to my knowledge. He was much affected. I felt tears dropping fast upon my hand. And looking towards him, saw them chasing one another in furrows over his dusty cheeks. He brushed them away suddenly with his left hand, and said to me in a voice tremulous with emotion, "Well, thank God, I don't know what it is to lose a battle; but certainly nothing can be more painful than to gain one with a loss of so many of one's friends."[23]

Whether in moments of epic triumph or inglorious defeat, great leaders are sensitive to the emotion of the moment. Their passion can be expressed either in celebration or sorrow almost simultaneously.

PASSION IS CONTAGIOUS

We have met many leaders of small inner-city churches and fledgling Christian organizations, and heard them enthusiastically tell of the marvelous things God was doing. Their ardor for what they sensed God was going to do through them inspired us to want to drop what we were doing and join with them. Such was the contagious nature of their zeal for God and His activity in their lives. Passion is not something you drum up within yourself. Either you have it or you don't. If you have lost it, it is imperative that you rediscover it.

A spiritual leader's passion comes from God. Spiritual leaders should be excited about what God is doing in their lives and exuberant about the possibilities of how God can impact others through them. Passion for God and His work gives leaders hope, even when circumstances appear grim.

God once made a promise to His people through His prophet Ezekiel: "I will give you a new heart and put a new spirit within you; I will take the heart of stone out of your flesh and give you a heart of flesh. I will put my Spirit within you" (Ezek. 36:26–27). Some of today's leaders desperately need God to do that for them. Over the years, their hearts have calcified under a steady stream of disappointments, criticisms, and failures. They have grown weary in well doing and have lost the heart to lead (Gal. 6:9). They still retain their leadership positions but they "retired" from leading long ago.

> **Defining moments of life shape the whole direction in which you go.**

JOSHUA WAS DECISIVE

Effective leadership relies heavily on the decision-making ability of the leader. Joshua was directing a precarious mission and handling the logistics of an extensive invading force. He could not afford to delay or waffle on his decisions. Like any good leader he learned to make important decisions in a timely manner.

Joshua showed no hesitancy when God came to him and officially appointed him as Israel's new leader. Joshua immediately ordered the entire army to break camp; he gave them three days to prepare to march (Josh. 1:11). When Joshua was forced to deal with treachery in his own camp, he quickly tackled it head-on (Josh. 7:10–26).

Joshua promptly took his mighty men of valor and set out on an all-night march, thirty-five kilometers uphill, after receiving a desperate appeal for help from his allies, the Gibeonites. His timely decision and sudden movement caught his enemies by surprise and helped secure him the victory (Josh. 10:6–10).

A PROMPT DECISION MUST BE A CAREFUL DECISION

The leaders of the tribes of Ephraim and Manasseh once approached Joshua with a complaint. They were populous tribes and believed they required more land than had been allotted to them (Josh. 17:14). Their request put Joshua in an awkward position. Appearing to show favoritism toward a tribe, regardless of its size, could have created resentment among the others.

To make matters worse, Ephraim was Joshua's tribe. If he gave them what they wanted, he could appear to be favoring his family, friends, and even himself. Joshua wisely offered to give them more land, but it would be hill country covered with forests and allegedly inhabited by giants (Josh. 17:15). None of the other tribes could begrudge such a gift!

When the tribal leaders complained of the hazards of occupying those lands, Joshua didn't budge. He had given them a fair and reasonable offer and he would not bend to any pressure. By deciding quickly and fairly, Joshua averted what could have been an extremely divisive controversy.

The Duke of Wellington made it his habit to always "Do the business of the day in the day."[24] Prompt action doesn't mean careless action. Robert E. Lee's son observed of his father: "One marked characteristic of my father was his habit of attending to all business matters promptly. He was never idle, and what he had to do he performed with care and precision."[25] These busy generals both understood the value of time.

Smart leaders know that time is a precious resource and they cannot afford to waste it by lingering over decisions that must be made immediately. In matters of war, a delayed decision can cost lives. Likewise, a careless decision can lead to great sorrow. It is important that good leaders remain diligent in their responsibilities and are always prepared to make timely decisions. Spiritual leaders should act immediately upon receiving a clear word from God. To hear from God and then delay responding is not prudence; it is disobedience.

JOSHUA TOOK TIME TO WORSHIP

No one could ever accuse Joshua of having an easy life! The accumulated weight of his demeaning beginnings as a slave, the nomadic years in the wilderness, and the arduous experience of leading the people into Canaan might have demoralized another leader. But Joshua's confidence in God never seemed to waver; he never lost sight of hope for the future, because he never strayed away from his relationship with God. At the outset of his work, God apprised him of the secret to success:

> This Book of the Law shall not depart from your mouth, but you shall meditate in it day and night, that you may observe to do according to all that is written in it. For then you will make your way prosperous, and then you will have good success. (Joshua 1:8)

As a military general, Joshua was a very busy man. He could have made excuses for not studying God's Word. He could have concluded that meditation was for those with the time for it. He could have questioned the relevancy of the Scriptures to a military officer, yet Joshua realized his walk with God had to come first. Not only would it determine his military success, his relationship with God would define every other form of success he would experience.

❧❧❧❧❧❧❧❧❧❧

His relationship with God would define every other form of success he would experience.

❧❧❧❧❧❧❧❧❧❧

In addition to keeping God's Word himself, Joshua expected his soldiers to do likewise. When Joshua prepared his soldiers to advance into enemy territory, he ordered: "Sanctify yourselves, for tomorrow the LORD will do wonders among you" (Josh. 3:5).

Even while the Canaanite armies were uniting and arming themselves to attack, Joshua took time to worship God and to renew his peoples' covenant with God (Josh. 8:30–35). Joshua understood that whatever else he might need to set aside in the urgency of the moment, time with God was still a priority.

BEGINNING THE DAY WITH GOD

A spiritual leader can never afford to neglect his walk with God. Everything he does as a leader hinges on his relationship with the Lord. Historically, great spiritual leaders have seized all the time necessary to ensure their devotional lives would be rich and full. Many rose early in the morning to begin their day with God.

The great Scottish revivalist, Duncan Campbell, wrote in his Bible the following quote from Lieutenant General Sir William Dobbie: "I have never found anything to compare with the morning-watch as a source of blessing when one meets God before meeting the world. It is a good thing to speak to Him before we speak to other people, to listen to His word before we listen to the voices of our fellow men."[26] Campbell always began his day with his Lord. As a result, his sermons carried with them an unmistakable divine anointing.

Beginning each day with significant time in God's presence is not the prerogative of only pastors and missionaries. Many corporate executives rise as early as four o'clock to allow for unhurried time with God. Busy leaders regularly schedule appointments with key personnel, board members, clients, or donors. These same leaders, if they are wise, will understand that time scheduled with God is the most important meeting on their calendar. Just as meeting with God sustained Joshua as an army commander, so communing with God will help people from all walks of life successfully meet the challenges of the day.

JOSHUA BLESSED HIS FOLLOWERS

Richard Nixon said of the American presidency, "This would be an easy job if you didn't have to deal with people."[27] Nixon was not known to have close friends while he led the nation. He regularly ate his lunch alone and scheduled Christmas parties at the White House for when he would be out of town. At one point his aides sought to develop a more "human" look for the president's image, so they brought a dog named King Timahoe into the Oval Office. However, even his pet wouldn't go near him unless they strung dog biscuits up to his desk![28]

Nixon failed to understand that leadership is all about people. It is influencing people for the corporate as well as the individual good.

Giving encouragement comes more naturally to some than to others. Although he was extremely successful on the battlefield, when the Duke of Wellington was asked if he had any regrets from his brilliant military career, he replied, "Yes, I should have given more praise."[29] But, as his biographer notes: "Like so many men who were themselves starved for affection as children, Wellington found it hard to lavish what he himself lacked."[30] It is well known that effective leaders are generally good at encouraging their followers, but we have seen that truly great leaders do more than encourage their people—they bless them.

Joshua led people to accomplish corporate goals but he did more than that. Joshua didn't use people; he blessed them. After Joshua led the Israelite forces to conquer Canaan, he released the tribes of Reuben, Gad, and Manasseh to return to their homes east of the Jordan River. Scripture indicates that before they departed, "Joshua blessed them" (Josh. 22:6). Perhaps Moses had taught Joshua the blessing God had taught him: "The LORD bless you and keep you; The LORD make His face shine upon you, And be gracious to you; The LORD lift up His countenance upon you, And give you peace" (Num. 6:24–26).

After all Joshua had accomplished as a general, he might have waited for the people to present *him* with a plaque of appreciation, or at least to give a speech or two in his honor. Instead, Joshua took that final opportunity to bless his followers. Joshua never manipulated people to achieve his goals; he sought what was best for the people.

It would not have been surprising if, after waiting forty years to finally lead, Joshua had prodded his troops forward posthaste to finish the job his predecessor had failed to accomplish. But throughout Joshua's leadership, he demonstrated a genuine concern for the spiritual well-being of his followers (Josh. 3:5; 5:2–9; 8:30–35; 23:1–24:28). Right to the end of Joshua's life he was urging his countrymen to walk closely with God. Even when it made no difference to his leadership, Joshua continued to express his concern for the people.

❧❧❧❧❧❧❧❧❧❧❧ Good leaders are master encouragers. But there is a difference between simply encouraging someone

> **Joshua didn't use people; he blessed them.**

and blessing them. A *good* leader will encourage someone to become a better worker; a *great* leader will bless someone so they become a better person.

❧❧❧❧❧❧❧❧❧❧❧ When you motivate people to work harder or to strive for excellence, you are helping them to become better followers, but you are not necessarily enabling them to become better people.

Perhaps in their efforts to produce more, church workers spend less and less time at home and their families are neglected. Or employees in the business world try to please the boss by taking work home every night. They may be highly motivated to accomplish more in their jobs but they will be failing at home where the cost is dear.

True spiritual leaders know how to bless people so that their lives are better for having worked with them. To bless people is to bring their names before God and to request God's best for them. The apostle Paul's prayers recorded in Scripture are wonderful blessings he asked God to accomplish in peoples' lives. In his letters he let people know specifically what he was asking God to do for them (Eph. 1:15–23; 3:14–21; Phil. 1:9–11; Col. 1:9–11).

Often as leaders ask God to bless their followers, God will move the leader to be a practical part of the blessing. This may mean occasionally nudging task-oriented staff to leave the office at the end of the day and go home to their families. Spiritual leaders may take time to enquire about their employees' families. Blessing people certainly involves praying regularly for them and maybe with them as they seek God's will for their lives. Leaders find ways to strengthen those in their organizations, and by extension to bless their families as well.

Many company employees or church volunteers work hard and give their best. After some have made many sacrifices "for the cause" they have been given a small plaque and ushered out the door. The world is full of people who feel they have been used and spent for the benefit of others. They watch the CEO receiving accolades for the company's success or their pastor taking credit for burgeoning church programs, and they realize their leaders have merely used them as steps to their own success.

> **To bless people is to bring their names before God and to request God's best for them.**

However, if you serve under a leader who knows how to bless others as God commanded, you should view the experience as an honor. If you had not been under the watchful, benevolent care of the leader God provided, you might not have weathered some of life's storms; you might never have grown as you have. Ulysses Grant said of Abraham Lincoln, "Mr. Lincoln gained influence over men by making them feel that it was a pleasure to serve him."[31]

ARE YOU BLESSING YOUR FOLLOWERS?

One test of whether you are blessing your followers is to watch how people respond to you (and to God) after they no longer work for you. Do they still keep in contact with you? Do they still seek your advice and welcome your input? Or do you hear through the grapevine that they are speaking ill of you to others? When you bless people, they will be your friends long after they are no longer your followers. And more importantly, they will be stronger Christians because of your influence. Many will go further in God's will because God honored your prayers. You will see what you prayed for—lived out and experienced in their lives.

The Duke of Marlborough and his wife Sarah seemed to have a knack for recognizing the rising stars of the future. There were many young soldiers and aspiring politicians who received encouragement and even financial aid from the Marlboroughs. Robert Warpole was a talented young noble in whom the Duke and his wife took special interest. Warpole was so grateful for the elder's patronage that he remained a devoted friend even when the Duke faced his greatest crisis.

Marlborough's powerful enemies, Robert Harley and Henry St. John, took control of the government and sought to disgrace Marlborough along with anyone who stood by him. Warpole refused to abandon his friend. He ultimately endured five humiliating months in the Tower of London rather than turn his back on the man who had blessed his life. Ultimately, Marlborough's enemies fell from power in disgrace, and Warpole eventually became one of the greatest prime ministers in British history.

Speaking of the intrigues Marlborough's enemies used against him, Winston Churchill noted they were "above all against Marlborough. Next in their animosity and fear stood Warpole. They knew they had struck down the great man of their day. It was only after some years that Harley and St. John realized they had incurred the implacable vengeance of the great man of the future."[32]

Fortuitously, perhaps, Marlborough had given his blessing to the most powerful man of the ensuing generation. Later, the Duchess of Marlborough gave property and ten thousand pounds to the young William Pitt who would also achieve renown as one of the great leaders in British history.[33] The Marlboroughs blessed those with whom they worked and, as a result, they had friends who were willing to face public scorn and imprisonment rather than abandon them in their time of need. Some of the people the Marlboroughs invested in eventually attained levels of power and influence the Duke never achieved himself. When you bless emerging leaders, you bless the future. It is at this point Joshua experienced his greatest failure, for he did not prepare for his own succession. Whereas Moses had a Joshua waiting in the wings as he retired from service, Joshua did not groom anyone to replace him. The chronicle of the book of Judges

When you bless emerging leaders, you bless the future.

provides a tragic commentary to the devastating consequences of Joshua's neglect.

CONCLUSION

Dwight Eisenhower said, "The one quality that can be developed by studious reflection and practice is the leadership of men."[34] It is true there are certain leadership skills that anyone can practice and incorporate into their leadership style. Learning to delegate, to communicate clearly, or to affirm others are all leadership practices that can be cultivated. In this regard, it is helpful to study the lives of people like Joshua to see what they did that made them such effective leaders.

SUBMISSION TO GOD

When it comes to the development of spiritual leaders, the most important element is the activity of God in a person's life. You cannot mimic that and it is not something you can achieve through practice or study. It comes through submission.

As people yield their lives entirely to God, God exercises His lordship over them and develops them into the leaders He wants them to be. God works in people's lives for *His* glory, not theirs. As we have seen, many people who are not practicing Christians exhibit good leadership traits. But Christians who allow God to mold their lives, experience a dimension of spiritual leadership not possible in the secular realm. Their lives are used to dramatically impact the kingdom of God.

> **God works in people's lives for *His* glory, not theirs.**

Spiritual leaders would do well to examine Joshua's leadership skills and to measure their own lives against his example. Then, in those areas where they fall short, they should humbly go before the Lord and ask Him to work those missing leadership traits into their lives. If God could take an ordinary man like Joshua and build into him the skills and character of a mighty spiritual leader, could He not do the same in your life?

JOSHUA'S LEADERSHIP PRINCIPLES

- Joshua grew during transitions.
- Joshua built on the past.
- Joshua was a teacher.
- Joshua used symbols.
- Joshua remained focused.
- Joshua had passion.
- Joshua was decisive.
- Joshua took time to worship.
- Joshua blessed his followers.

QUESTIONS FOR CONSIDERATION

1. Do you consider yourself an effective leader? Why or why not?
2. What is God presently doing in your life to make you a better leader?
3. Are you currently in a transition time? How are you handling it?
4. How are you building on the past of the organization you are leading? How are you building on what God taught you in the past?
5. What symbols or stories could you use with your people to clearly communicate the values and mission of your organization?
6. Have you lost your focus? How are you relentlessly pursuing your organization's mission?
7. Are you passionate about the task God has given you or have you lost your enthusiasm? Are you merely going through the motions as a leader?

8. How are you ensuring your relationship with God remains paramount regardless of the demands on your time?

9. How are you blessing those with whom you work? How are people better for having worked with you?

CONCLUSION

THE WORLD WAS NEVER THE SAME after God touched Joshua's life. God took a man of no worldly consequence and made him into someone history cannot ignore. Joshua did not have extraordinary intelligence, unusual physical strength, or a remarkable appearance—nothing set him apart as destined for any degree of success. In fact, he was decidedly ordinary. What does stand out about him is his willingness to allow God to work so thoroughly in and through his life. God had total access to Joshua's life. Joshua's generation reaped the benefits and we are still experiencing the results thousands of years later.

Before time, God intended to free a people from their bondage. Further, He planned to establish a special holy nation that would spiritually illuminate the rest of the world. To that kingdom of priests, God would send His only Son as the Savior for every person who would trust in Him. All this was in God's mind and heart before the land of Canaan was even formed. When the time came to put His plan into motion, God sought those He would use as leaders. First God used the patriarchs Abraham, Isaac, and Jacob. Four hundred years later God called Moses. After Moses led the people as far as God would allow, God called Joshua.

Had Joshua lived a century earlier, we would probably never have heard of him. But in God's providence, Joshua was born at a critical moment in history. Every person's life intersects history—only a few impact it. How Joshua chose to respond to God would determine whether God used him in His plan. Joshua had a tender heart toward God. If God was looking for an instrument, Joshua was eager to be taken into his Master's hand. Joshua's availabil-

Every person's life intersects history— only a few impact it.

ity to God led him to experience the profound joy of influencing his world and blessing God's people.

God did not simply transform Joshua into a godly individual. He fashioned him into a spiritual leader. Leaders don't live for themselves; they live for others. Their lives raise everyone around them to heights they would not otherwise achieve.

University of Oxford philosopher, Isaiah Berlin, said Winston Churchill was "a leader who imposed his 'imagination and his will upon his countrymen,' idealizing them 'with such intensity that in the end they approached his ideal and began to see themselves as he saw them.' In doing so he 'transformed cowards into brave men, and so fulfilled the purpose of shining armour.'"[1] That is what leaders do. They move people from where they are to where they must be. Spiritual leaders take people from where they are to the place God intends for them. Joshua did that.

> **Spiritual leaders take people from where they are to the place God intends for them.**

Every generation waits to see who is willing to be its spiritual leaders. God's plan from eternity included our age. Surely God intends to do a great work and liberate people in this day. There are multitudes of people who need someone to help move them from where they are to the place God has for them.

There is a price to be paid in becoming a spiritual leader; otherwise, there would be many more. Many Christians are satisfied with merely living out their individual existences, pursuing temporal pleasures, enjoying life to its fullest, and then departing this life to reside with God for eternity. Some are seduced into attempting to impact the world for their own gain or their own fame.

Deep within the hearts of others, however, is a sincere desire to live in a manner that makes a difference. These men and women want to leave the world a better place than when they first came into it. They know, as Joshua did, that they can do nothing of lasting significance apart from God. So they yield their lives to God and humbly ask Him to do whatever He must do to

A humble, committed, passionate servant of God is a perfect conduit for God to release His unparalleled power.

make them suitable instruments in His hands. A humble, committed, passionate servant of God is a perfect conduit for God to release His unparalleled power.

We have studied the lives of scores of history's leaders. Some pursued fame for themselves; others sought to glorify God. Eternity will prove who made the better investment. In analyzing the fascinating life of Napoleon, historian Paul Johnson concluded: "We have to learn again the central lesson of history: that all forms of greatness, military and administrative, nation and empire building, are as nothing—indeed are perilous in the extreme—without a humble and a contrite heart."[2] Joshua had such a heart and God used him mightily.

APPENDIX A
MAP OF THE EXODUS FROM EGYPT

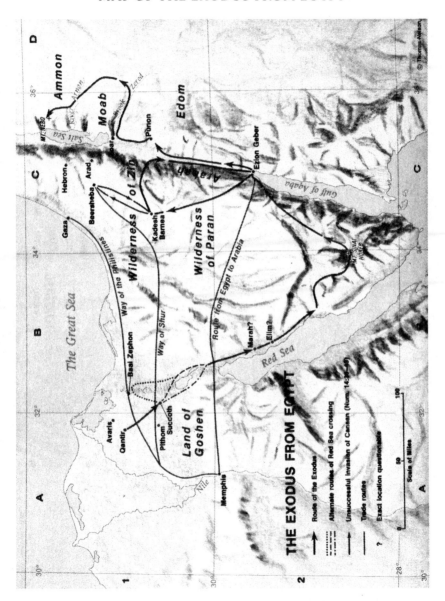

THE EXODUS FROM EGYPT

→ Route of the Exodus

┈┈┈ Alternate routes of Red Sea crossing

↑ Unsuccessful invasion of Canaan (Num 14:39-45)

| Trade routes

? Exact location questionable

Scale of Miles
0   50   100

APPENDIX B
MAP OF THE CONQUEST OF CANAAN

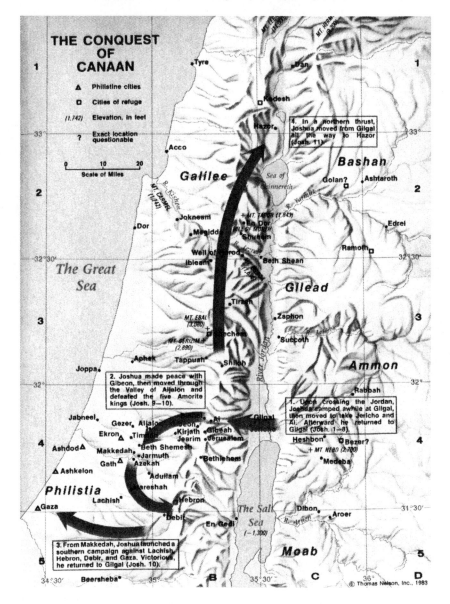

NOTES

INTRODUCTION

1. Brian Edwards, *Revival! A People Saturated with God* (Darlington, England: Evangelical Press, 1990; reprint ed., 1994), 47.
2. Christian Meier, *Caesar*, (London: Fontana Books, 1996) 413.
3. William Manchester, *The Last Lion: Winston Spencer Churchill, Alone 1932–1940* (New York: Dell Publishing, 1988; reprint ed., 1989), 676.

CHAPTER 1

1. Jean Edward Smith, *Grant* (New York: Simon and Schuster, 2001; Touchstone Edition, 2002), 91.
2. Ibid., 107.
3. James MacGregor Burns, *Leadership* (New York: Harper Torchbooks, 1978), 285.
4. Richard Holmes, *Wellington: The Iron Duke* (London: Harper Collins, 2003), 8–9.
5. D. A. Land, *I Was with Patton: First-Person Accounts of WWII in George Patton's Command* (St. Paul, Minnesota: MBI Publishing, 2002), 292.

CHAPTER 2

1. Willard Sterne Randall, *George Washington: A Life* (New York: Henry Holt and Co., 1997), 143.
2. Ibid, 283.
3. H. W. Brands, *The First American: The Life and Times of Benjamin Franklin* (New York: Anchor Books, 2002), 101.
4. Smith, *Grant*, 24.
5. Laurie Nadel, *The Great Streams of History: A Biography of Richard M. Nixon* (New York: Macmillan Publishing Company, 1991), 6, 17.
6. Ibid., 18.
7. Ibid., 31.
8. Stephen E. Ambrose, *Eisenhower: Soldier and President* (New York: Simon and Schuster, 1990; Touchstone Edition, 1991), 526.
9. Richard Reeves, *President Kennedy: Profile in Power* (New York: Simon and Schuster, 1993; Touchstone Edition, 1994), 278.
10. Ibid., 40.
11. Holmes, *Wellington: The Iron Duke* 32.
12. Land, *I Was with Patton*, 104.
13. Ambrose, *Eisenhower: Soldier and President*, 82.

CHAPTER 3

1. Paul Johnson, *Napoleon* (New York: Penguin Books, 2002), 8.
2. Ibid., xi-xii.
3. Holmes, *Wellington: The Iron Duke*, 197.
4. Johnson, *Napoleon*, 59.
5. Ibid., 133.

6. Holmes, *Wellington: The Iron Duke,* 108, 184.

7. Ambrose, *Eisenhower: Soldier and President,* 54.

8. Alison Weir, *Elizabeth the Queen* (London: Jonathan Cape Ltd., 1998; Pimlico Edition, 1999), 19.

9. Ibid., 436.

10. Robert E. Lee, *The Recollections and Letters of Robert E. Lee,* (New York: Konecky and Konecky, n.d.), 94.

11. Ibid., 95.

12. Ibid., 94.

13. Reeves, *President Nixon: Alone in the White House* (New York: Simon and Schuster, 2001; Touchstone Edition, 2002), 206.

CHAPTER 4

1. Duncan Campbell, *The Nature of God-Sent Revival* (Vinton, Virginia: Christ Life Publications, n.d.), 23.

2. Duncan Campbell, *The Price and Power of Revival: Lessons from the Hebrides Awakening* (Edinburgh: Faith Mission, n.d.), 30.

3. "Revival in the Hebrides" (1949) http://www.gospelcom.net/npc/Campbell.html

4. Campbell, *The Nature of God-Sent Revival,* 27.

5. Randall, *George Washington,* 96.

6. Meier, *Caesar,* 305.

7. J. R. Hamilton, *Alexander the Great* (Pittsburgh: University of Pittsburgh Press, 1973; reprint ed., 1982), 127.

8. Smith, *Grant,* 159-160.

9. Manchester, *The Last Lion: Winston Spencer Churchill, Alone 1932-1940,* 25.

10. Brands, *The First American: The Life and Times of Benjamin Franklin,* 41.

11. Manchester, *The Last Lion: Winston Spencer Churchill, Alone 1932-1940,* 618.

12. Ambrose, *Eisenhower: Soldier and President,* 293.

13. Ibid., 278.

14. Ibid., 223.

15. John Pollock, *Moody: A Biography* (Grand Rapids: Baker Books, 1963; reprint ed., 1992), 193.

16. Ibid., 261.

17. See our book, *Hearing God's Voice* (Nashville: Broadman and Holman, 2002) for a comprehensive discussion of how to hear God's voice.

18. Two books we would recommend are: Wesley Duewel, *Heroes of the Holy Life* (Grand Rapids: Zondervan, 2002) and V. Raymond Edman, *They Found the Secret: Twenty Lives that Reveal a Touch of Eternity,* (Grand Rapids: Zondervan, 1960; reprint ed., 1984).

19. Weir, *Elizabeth the Queen,* 14, 229.

20. Manchester, *The Last Lion: Winston Spencer Churchill, Alone 1932-1940,* 536.

21. Ambrose, *Eisenhower: Soldier and President,* 299.

CHAPTER 5

1. Weir, *Elizabeth the Queen,* 299.

2. Ibid., 256.

3. Ibid., 255.

4. These are: *Your Church Experiencing God* and *What's So Spiritual About Your Gifts?*

5. Holmes, *Wellington: The Iron Duke,* xvi, 254.

6. Elizabeth Longford, *Victoria R.I.* (London: Weidenfeld and Nicolson, 1964; Abacus Publishing Edition, 2000), 439.

7. David McCasland, *Oswald Chambers: Abandoned to God* (Grand Rapids: Discovery House Publishers, 1993), 109.

CHAPTER 6

1. Winston S. Churchill, *Marlborough: His Life and Times Book One* (London: George C. Harrap and Co., Ltd. 1936-7; reprint ed. Chicago: University of Chicago Press, 2002), 430-431.
2. Ibid., 571.
3. Johnson, *Napoleon*, 65.
4. Weir, *Elizabeth the Queen*, 227.
5. Longford, *Victoria R.I.*, 415.
6. Meier, *Caesar*, 156.
7. Ibid., 33.
8. Weir, *Elizabeth the Queen*, 1.
9. Ibid., 16.
10. Ulysses S. Grant, *Personal Memoirs of U.S. Grant* (New York: Konecky and Konecky, 1885; reprint ed. n.d.), 30.
11. Pollock, *Moody*, 17-18.
12. Smith, *Grant*, 92-93.
13. Reeves, *President Nixon: Alone in the White House*, 35.
14. Ibid., 36.
15. Churchill, *Marlborough Book One*, 905.
16. Ibid., *Book Two*, 154.
17. Holmes, *Wellington: The Iron Duke*, 277-278.
18. Ibid., 278.
19. Lee, *Recollections and Letters*, 75.
20. Smith, *Grant*, 7.
21. Joseph J. Ellis, *Founding Brothers: The Revolutionary Generation* (New York: Vintage Books, 2000), 130.
22. David McCullough, *John Adams* (New York: Simon and Schuster, 2001; Touchstone Edition, 2002), 413.
23. Ellis, *Founding Brothers*, 130.
24. Johnson, *Napoleon*, 11.
25. Ibid., 42.
26. Hamilton, *Alexander the Great*, 138-141.
27. Ibid., 148.
28. Meier, *Caesar*, 444, 474.
29. Churchill, *Marlborough, Book Two*, 861-862.
30. Tom Pocock, *Horatio Nelson* (London: Cassell Publishers, 1987; Brockhampton Press Edition, 1999), 165.
31. Lee, *Recollections and Letters*, 124.
32. Smith, *Grant*, 281.
33. Ibid., 417-418.
34. Churchill, *Marlborough, Book Two*, 796.
35. Ibid., *Book One*, 740.
36. Weir, *Elizabeth the Queen*, 372.

CHAPTER 7

1. Courtney Anderson, *To The Golden Shore: The Life of Adoniram Judson* (n.p.: Little, Brown and Company, 1956; reprint ed., Grand Rapids: Zondervan, 1972); See also,

Wesley L. Duewel, *Heroes of the Holy Life: Biographies of Fully Devoted Followers of Christ* (Grand Rapids: Zondervan, 2002), 102-121.

2. Howard and Geraldine Taylor, Edited by Gregg Lewis, *Hudson Taylor's Spiritual Secret* (n.p.: China Inland Mission, 1932; reprint ed., Grand Rapids: Discovery House Publishers, 1990), 226.

3. Ibid., 224.

4. George Muller, *The Autobiography of George Muller*, Diana L. Matisko ed., (Springdale, Pennsylvania: Whitaker House, 1984), 101.

5. Land, *I Was with Patton*, 183.

6. Ibid., 185.

7. Holmes, *Wellington: The Iron Duke*, 246.

8. Pocock, *Horatio Nelson*, 233.

9. Ibid., 236-237.

10. Hamilton, *Alexander the Great*, 165.

11. Ambrose, *Eisenhower: Soldier and President*, 112.

12. Billy Graham, *Just As I Am: The Autobiography of Billy Graham* (New York: Harper Collins, 1997; Harper Paperbacks Edition, 1998), 439.

13. Pollock, *Moody*, 139.

14. Smith, *Grant*, 372.

15. McCasland, *Oswald Chambers: Abandoned to God*, 194.

16. Taylor, *Hudson Taylor's Spiritual Secret*, 181.

17. Ron Owens, *They Could Not Stop the Music: The Life and Witness of Georgy Slesarev* (Kingsport, Tennessee: Fresh Springs Publications, 2000), 88-89.

CHAPTER 8

1. See Henry and Richard Blackaby, *Spiritual Leadership: Moving People on to God's Agenda* (Nashville: Broadman and Holman, 2001).

2. Churchill, *Marlborough, Book Two*, 357.

3. Ibid., 339.

4. Ambrose, *Eisenhower: Soldier and President*, 129.

5. Manchester, *The Last Lion: Winston Spencer Churchill, Alone 1932-1940*, 494.

6. Weir, *Elizabeth the Queen*, 250.

7. Ibid., 226.

8. Randall, *George Washington*, 329.

9. Ellis, *Founding Brothers*, 124.

10. Ibid.

11. Ambrose, *Eisenhower: Soldier and President*, 546.

12. Longford, *Victoria R.I.*, 72.

13. Smith, *Grant*, 269.

14. Ibid., 108.

15. Ibid.

16. Ibid., 200.

17. Ibid.

18. Ibid., 232.

19. Holmes, *Wellington: The Iron Duke*, 42.

20. Manchester, *The Last Lion: Winston Spencer Churchill, Alone 1932-1940*, 127.

21. Ambrose, *Eisenhower: Soldier and President*, 82.

22. Churchill, *Marlborough, Book Two*, 846-857.

23. Longford, *Victoria R.I.*, 73.

24. Pocock, *Horatio Nelson*, 317-318.
25. McCullough, *John Adams*, 529.
26. Brands, *The First American: The Life and Times of Benjamin Franklin*, 328, 528, 645.
27. Manchester, *The Last Lion: Winston Spencer Churchill, Alone 1932-1940*, 253-254.
28. Ibid., 252.
29. Lee, *The Recollections and Letters of Robert E. Lee*, 73-74.
30. Ambrose, *Eisenhower: Soldier and President*, 144.
31. Holmes, *Wellington: The Iron Duke*, 262.
32. Churchill, *Marlborough, Book Two*, 365.
33. Ibid., 391.
34. Taylor, *Hudson Taylor's Spiritual Secret*, 137-141.
35. Muller, *The Autobiography of George Muller*, 47.
36. Reeves, *President Kennedy: Profile of Power*, 261.
37. Randall, *George Washington*, 194.
38. Ellis, *Founding Brothers*, 160.

CHAPTER 9
1. Meier, *Caesar*, 306.
2. Ibid., 309.
3. Ibid., 330.
4. Ibid., 397.
5. Ibid., 459.
6. Ibid., 132.
7. Land, *I Was with Patton*, 297.
8. Smith, *Grant*, 420.
9. Weir, *Elizabeth the Queen*, 224.
10. Ibid.
11. Ibid., 236.
12. Longford, *Victoria R.I.*, 331.
13. Pocock, *Horatio Nelson*, 64-65.
14. Ibid., 65.
15. Randall, *George Washington*, 396.
16. Ibid., 396.
17. Smith, *Grant*, 239.
18. Ibid., 15.
19. Ibid.
20. Ibid., 301.
21. Pollock, *Moody*, 77.
22. Smith, *Grant*, 292.
23. Holmes, *Wellington: The Iron Duke*, 250.
24. Ibid., 86.
25. Lee, *The Recollections and Letters of Robert E. Lee*, 89.
26. Quoted in Wesley Duewel, *Heroes of the Holy Life* (Zondervan, 2002), 34.
27. Reeves, *President Nixon: Alone in White House*, 326.
28. Ibid., 31, 35.
29. Holmes, *Wellington: The Iron Duke*, 251.
30. Ibid., 202.
31. Grant, *The Personal Memoirs of Ulysses S. Grant*, 655.
32. Churchill, *Marlborough, Book Two*, 927.

33. Ibid., 1039-1040.
34. Ambrose, *Eisenhower: Soldier and President*, 81.

CONCLUSION
1. Quoted in Manchester, *The Last Lion: Winston Spencer Churchill, Alone 1932-1940*, 682.
2. Johnson, *Napoleon*, 186-187.

ABOUT THE AUTHORS

HENRY BLACKABY and his wife Marilynn have five children, all of whom are actively serving in full-time Christian ministry. They also have fourteen grandchildren. Dr. Blackaby graduated from the University of British Columbia and Golden Gate Baptist Theological Seminary. He has also been granted four honorary doctoral degrees. He has authored numerous books, many with his children. His best-known work is *Experiencing God: Knowing and Doing the Will of God*. He previously coauthored eight books with his son Richard, including *Experiencing God: Day by Day; Spiritual Leadership: Moving People on to God's Agenda;* and *Hearing God's Voice*. Dr. Blackaby speaks worldwide and regularly consults with Christian CEOs in America on issues related to spiritual leadership.

RICHARD BLACKABY is the oldest son of Henry and Marilynn. He previously coauthored eight books with his father, including, *Experiencing God: Day by Day; Spiritual Leadership;* and *Hearing God's Voice*. He is married to Lisa and has three teenage children, Mike, Daniel, and Carrie. Richard was the pastor of Friendship Baptist Church, Winnipeg, before becoming the president of the Canadian Southern Baptist Seminary in Cochrane, Alberta, Canada. He travels widely, speaking on the subject of spiritual leadership.

BIBLICAL LEGACY SERIES

Prepared to Be God's Vessel: How God Can Use an Obedient Life to Bless Others
Henry Blackaby and his daughter Carrie Webb Blackaby show through the life of Mary how God can use any woman—regardless of stature or abilities—if her heart is fully committed to Him.
Hardcover ISBN: 0-7852-6207-5

Anointed to Be God's Servants:
How God Blesses Those Who Serve Him
Through the life of Paul, readers will learn of the critical role that supporting companions play in God's kingdom.
Hardcover ISBN: 0-7852-6205-9; Workbook ISBN: 0-7852-6206-7

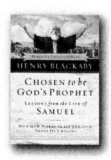

Chosen to Be God's Prophet: How God Works in and Through Those He Chooses
By studying Samuel's life, readers learn to recognize their own defining moments, and see how moments often defined in crises are simply the voice of God, calling us to His purpose.
Hardcover ISBN: 0-7852-6555-4; Trade paper ISBN: 0-7852-7510-X
Workbook ISBN: 0-7852-6557-0

Created to Be God's Friend: How God Shapes Those He Loves
Using the life of Abraham as his palette, best-selling author Henry Blackaby shows how God shapes and sculpts men and women so that eventually they become His friends.
Hardcover ISBN: 0-7852-6389-6; Trade paper ISBN: 0-7852-7532-0
Workbook ISBN: 0-7852-6391-8

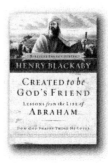

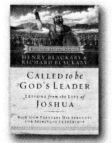

Called to Be God's Leader: How God Prepares His Servants for Spiritual Leadership
In *Called to Be God's Leader*, readers will see how God applies leadership principles in the life of the great biblical leader Joshua.
Hardcover ISBN: 0-7852-6203-2; Workbook ISBN: 0-7852-6204-0